Jean Wilson

WEAVING IS FUN

A guide for teachers, children & beginning weavers · About yarns, baskets, cloth & tapestry

VAN NOSTRAND REINHOLD COMPANY New York
STUDIO VISTA LIMITED London

TO RON

My grateful thanks go to all the weavers who so generously shared weavings and experiences so I could pass them along to you; read the names in the text and captions as a list of the people who helped make this book possible.

Good photographs are of prime importance, so my sincere thanks to Kent Kammerer, whose excellent photographs — and understanding and patience — contributed so much;

To William Eng, whose fine photography enhances this book, as it did my first one;

To the two artists whose drawings add interest: Mary Bassetti, for her charming pencil sketches and Michael Mosier for his meticulous ink drawings.

And abundant appreciation and thanks to all those teachers who so generously shared ideas and experiences with me; since this book is aimed at teachers of beginning weaving, as well as beginners, their cooperation was invaluable, especially the contribution of Tom Reeder, who inspired his fifth graders to really have fun weaving. To Larry Metcalf, whose teaching and class results contributed so much, to Jeannine Heroux of the Renton School District, who found so much material for me, to Betsey Bess, Virginia Harvey, and all the rest of you — my sincere thanks for the interest and help given.

Weaving really is fun — and I hope this book will prove it to you.

Jean Wilson
Bellevue, Washington
March, 1970

Also by Jean Wilson
WEAVING IS FOR ANYONE

Van Nostrand Reinhold Company Regional Offices:
New York   Cincinnati   Chicago   Millbrae   Dallas

Copyright © 1971 by Litton Educational Publishing, Inc.
Library of Congress Catalog Card Number: 74-1268-77
UK SBN: 289-70196-1   US ISBN: 0-442-29527-8

Designed by Jean Callan King

Published by Van Nostrand Reinhold Company, 450 West 33rd Street, New York, N.Y. 10001
and simultaneously in Canada by Van Nostrand Reinhold Company Ltd., Toronto
Published in London by Studio Vista Limited, Blue Star House, Highgate Hill, London N19
3   5   7   9   11   13   15   16   14   12   10   8   6   4   2

CONTENTS

Chapter numbers in the text were woven by the author especially for this book.

FOREWORD

As I study and try techniques, and read the history of weaving and basketry, I keep thinking over and over again — "this one technique is a whole book" there is so much to say, so much to share with you. It required strong discipline not to go down too many by-ways, to wander too far. If this book has a mission, it is to bring you a related assortment of techniques and materials and hope that you will become intrigued enough to search out the great amount of material available — items in museums and other collections, current showings of textiles, the new books and excellent craft magazines.

The ground swell of rising interest in crafts continues, and textiles are high on the crest; more and more craftsmen are turning to weaving, stitchery, macramé, batik, tie-dye, and related textile crafts. The trends have been interesting to watch over the past twenty years or so. For a time, everyone was "doing ceramics" or "making mosaics" — comparatively few were weaving or embroidering. With the blooming of craft books and other publications, workshops and conferences, there is again a great surge toward the textile crafts. Craftsmen and designers are trying all media, and each gives something to the other. Sculptors are weaving and knotting in 3D. Knitters are doing curtains and wall hangings. Artists are painting, tying and dying, and stitching textiles. Exciting happenings result from this blending and melding of crafts. It is all part of the disappearance of past boundaries which had tended to keep a craftsman in one field; the urge now is to hurry up and try the whole range of crafts, not just one.

Approach creative work with the imagination and the freedom of a child, with joy in the doing of it. The important part is that human hands have manipulated raw material and left an impression. Abilities vary, so handwork varies in qualities of design and craftsmanship. The thing is, if you have the desire to create — do it!

You become a creative, thinking weaver-designer when:
• After dutifully weaving samples, learning where and how the yarn moves, what effects are produced by colors and textures,
• You wonder what the effect would be with a different size or spin of yarn, or a different color replacing that in certain areas, or wonder what a change in the scale of the design would do.
• Then — you do some sampling to see.

In our society much emphasis is put on monetary value — will it sell? Will it win a prize? Primitive people created with joy and took endless time for perfection. How often now, seeing a charming weaving or carving, you think it is lovely and well-done, but then, when you see a fine old original, you realize what true, dedicated craftsmanship really is. Study our photograph of the exquisite brocade finger-nail weaving (figure 1-29). You will recognize at once that this must have taken much time, great skill and incredible patience. We speak of "touristy" things — crafts turned out in quantity in a hurry, to sell. Such designs are usually based on sound, functional-use designs and methods of construction, and although they are usually crafted using handed-down methods, tools, and materials, the sincere, careful, and prideful craftsmanship is gone; it is apparent that each separate piece was not done lovingly, but was put together at so many per day for so many cents each.

Just for fun, weave a detailed, carefully thought-out tapestry. Not for an exhibit, not for sale, but just for the pure joy of creating something with your hands to the best of your ability. The feeling of pleasure and accomplishment is a good one!

Weaving is often likened to music — there is rhythm in the repetition of the yarns and patterns, rhythm in the actual weaving, the throwing of the shuttle and the beating. Like a melody in music, colors and patterns weave in and out and intermingle. In older days, weavers had a musical measurement of time for weaving. It took so many songs to weave a length, and the weaver achieved rhythm and pleasure in the weaving by singing along the way.

Handicrafts are a natural bridge back to earlier days when almost everything was made by hand, often at home. Brides prepared flax, made linen thread, and wove sheets, towels, and counterpanes for the new home. Bridegrooms made furniture and tools, sometimes made the wooden and clay dishes, and built the house itself. Now, with no real need for making basic necessities, we can do handicrafts for the fun of it — for the joy of creating. And there should be no real pressure for hurried planning and rush work.

PREFACE

A WORD ABOUT LOOMS

Presumably a book on weaving should start with information about looms, for to do any weaving at all, you must have some kind of a loom or holder for your warp. After a great deal of thought, however, and perusal of chapter titles in the deluge of new books about weaving and reprints of old ones, I concluded that the subject of looms has been more than adequately covered. I have preferred, in this book, to use the space for additional photographs of textiles to spur you on, to give you ideas, to tell you something about yarns and where they come from, limiting the subject of looms to just a few simple looms at work, including a truly wonderful new concept of warping on a newly marketed loom, and to providing help for teachers and beginning weavers by suggested sampling on a frame or cardboard loom, along with classroom experiences. These directions have been used in several elementary grades and checked out by teachers on all levels from grade schools through university. I hope they work for you.

THE RIGHT CRAFT TOOLS

Handcraft tools are extremely important to a craftsman. The right tool may make the difference between a good, workmanlike job and an inferior one. A loom must be as personally suitable and comfortable for the weaver as a chair or a good working light. There are floor looms, table looms, backstrap looms, all sizes and kinds of frame looms and vertical looms. There are looms appropriate for each kind of weaving. Your floor space, the length of your arms, the kind of weaving you are most interested in, how much money you can spend, even your own patience, attention span, and tolerance for slow detail work — all of these must be considered if you are to be a happy, productive designer-weaver. One word of advice: Don't invest in a large, expensive multiple-harness loom until you have had a chance to try out other looms. Be sure you find the right one for you. Eager weavers are often baffled by too large and elaborate a loom, and defeated before they start.

On page 138 you will find a brief list of useful reference publications. These will familiarize you with many different types of looms and weaving.

A NEW LOOM IDEA

A new idea in loom design is incorporated in the Pioneer Loom made by Northwest Looms. To help spread the word, we are including an illustration of this new loom. Reports are favorable, and you may want to learn more about it. Information is available from Northwest Looms, Box 241 Coburg, Oregon, 97401.

The idea was developed by a weaver, Dorothy Tow, to save time in designing on the loom and to permit fast and easy warping and warp changes. Heddles and reed are open at the top and warping is done with a continuous yarn directly from spools. This eliminates pre-measuring and all of the equipment needed for warping and threading. The back beam extends, as well as the front, allowing for a maximum continuous warp of about two-and-a-half yards. A warp up to eight yards, measured in the conventional manner, can also be used on this table loom. An excellent little loom for use in classes. It stores easily, is compact, well-built, and saves time in threading the reed and heddles. It may have from two to eight harnesses. A very useful loom for designing and sampling.

The Pioneer Loom — This loom, featuring the open heddle and reed idea patented by Dorothy Tow, is so named because it is a new concept in the world of handweaving. Designed and manufactured by Mr. and Mrs. Malcolm Campbell, an architect and a weaver.

From source to yarn to fabric

After early man settled down and began to learn about his environment and feel at home in it, he became adept at using the raw materials he found at hand. As his requirements for living increased, his inventiveness and ability also increased; he discovered how to devise containers and carriers, how to build shelters to protect him from weather and wild animals, and how to fashion clothing. When he discovered how to twist plant fibers and animal hairs to make a continuous strand, he was well on his way to weaving with long yarns, making a fabric out of small units of material.

The structure of a woven fabric begins with loose fibers twisted into long flexible, strands, which are interlaced to form a textile. Whatever raw material you start with, it must be drawn out into a strand of yarn. Natural yarns are so called because they are made from growing materials; animal wools and hair, fibers of plants such as cotton and flax, and silk filament produced by silkworms. Man-made yarns are those made from various inert materials treated chemically and converted into threads through factory procedures, producing yarns of rayon, nylon, glass, and dozens of synthetic combinations.

Many different kinds of equipment and processes are required to create a long, flexible strand of yarn whether it is made from a growing material, such as an animal coat, or a plant, or from inert substances.

Steps in early textile making depicted in ancient tomb drawings and in scenes on antique pottery give us clues as to what fibers the early weavers worked with. A drop spindle signifies wool. The spindle resting in a bowl or on the ground indicates that cotton is probably being spun. We can conclude this from the knowledge that wool clings to itself and can withstand a dropped weight, whereas cotton fibers are short and smooth and, until spun, cannot sustain a strong pull without coming apart.

The history, steps of preparation, language, tools, and the romance of discovery and progress in the story of creating yarns would fill several books. Regretfully, we can only touch on a few of the high spots, but we hope to stir your interest by giving you a broad picture of how yarns are created. If you would like to learn more about processes, we refer you to the list of useful reference publications on page 138.

Raw fiber is the term used for wool just as it is taken from the sheep, cotton just as it is picked from the boll (seedpod), silk as it is reeled from the cocoon, and so on. The material must be harvested, cleaned, combed or straightened in preparation for spinning.

In our day of machines and the need to manufacture large quantities of yarns and cloth with great speed, obviously hand processes cannot be used. However, to help you visualize how yarns are created, we show some of the main steps between the raw material and the finished yarn as done by hand with simple devices so you may more easily appreciate how these basic methods are speeded up by machinery. Hand methods are still used by individual weavers who prefer to begin by actually making their own yarn. There are still places where the production is small and where people need and want to do the work; here time stretches to allow the use of hand processes. Our sketches recall a few unhurried old ways. The happenings between gathering raw material and transforming it into strands of yarn are many and varied. Each kind of raw material has its own course to follow.

The illustrations that follow will give you a sampling of the different look and uses of the many fibers available to weavers.

1-1. Toy llamas on an Irish sheepskin, guarding llama and alpaca yarns. Tiny handwoven saddle blankets indicate that they are beasts of burden. (Photograph by Kent Kammerer.)

1-2. Handspun and unspun wools, cotton, and jute yarns. (Photograph by Kent Kammerer.)

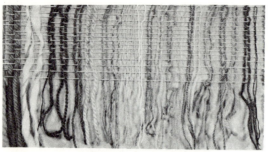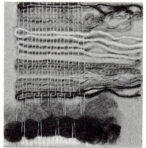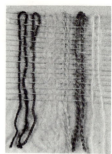

Above left: 1-3. Wool yarns. High bulk two ply, thick and thin spun, single, double, and triple ply. *Center:* 1-4. Wool yarns. Unspun at the left, all others are handspun. *Right:* 1-5. Wool and Mohair. Looped, hairy, double and single ply. (Photographs by William Eng.)

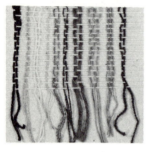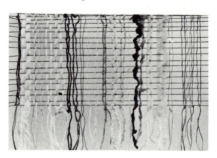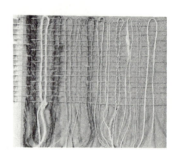

Above left: 1-6. Combinations of wool and other animal fibers: camel hair, alpaca, llama, mountain sheep from Iceland. *Center:* 1-7. Cotton yarn. Carpet warp, roving, seine twine, rug yarn, fine and coarse, one, two, or three ply, flake, nub, ratiné, thick and thin handspun Mexican chenille, two sizes. To the right, mercerized cottons. *Right:* 1-8. Linen. Tow, smooth, rough, textured, thick, and thin. (Photographs by William Eng.)

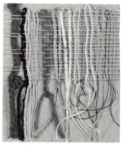

Above left: 1-9. Silk. Raw silk, smooth, shiny, dull, nubby, bouclé, single, double, and triple ply. *Center:* 1-10. Plant fibers. Jute, hemp, sisal. *Right:* 1-11. Man-made fibers. Orlon, rayon, saran, nylon, acrylic. *Below:* 1-12. Man-made fibers in combination with other fibers. Rayon with cotton, wool, linen, jute. (Photographs by William Eng.)

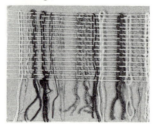

1-13. Wool yarns with a shiny synthetic straw yarn. (Photograph by Kent Kammerer.)

1-14. A variety of yarns and spools. (Photograph by Kent Kammerer.)

ALL KINDS OF YARN

Figures 1-3 through 1-12 show examples of many kinds of yarn. We wove them into a warp, with ends hanging loose, so you could see their different characteristics. Some hang straight and smooth, some curl and twist, while others are stiff and spiky. Different spins are included, but these are only a fraction of the vast array of novelty yarns and range of sizes, the number of plys and twists available; there are smooth, dull, shiny, single ply, tightly spun double ply, nubby, harsh, soft, loopy, crisp! Our photographs show all the types of fibers discussed.

Yarns are wound in a number of forms for sale — spools, cones, balls, hanks, and skeins, large and small. Large cones may weigh from one to three pounds. Small balls may weigh only one ounce.

Wool is obtained mainly from sheep, but llamas, camels, goats, shaggy dogs, Angora rabbits, and other animals also provide wool or hair that can be spun into yarn. Hair-like wools are composed of down, which grows close to the body, and guard hairs that extend beyond the down and form another layer. Sometimes sheep wool is combined with other wools and animal hair to make yarn with a texture different from yarn made entirely of one kind of fiber. This yarn may be stronger, softer, fuzzier, or longer-wearing than that made of a single kind of fiber. Sometimes blends are made to get a new, natural color. A natural-color yarn may be carded with a dyed yarn for a soft, subtle shade impossible to get by dyeing only.

ABOUT SHEEP AND WOOL

Sheep are perhaps the most familiar and appealing of the yarn animals. We learn about them early in nursery rhymes about Mary's little lamb and Baa Baa Black Sheep. Having tended and nurtured them, worked with their wool in all phases of carding, dyeing, spinning, and weaving, I find their product is endlessly interesting and more than satisfying.

Wool — and every natural fiber — varies a great deal in quality and characteristics. Wool can be coarse, wiry, soft, curly, long staple or short. Each individual animal grows a variety of qualities on various parts of its body, suitable for different uses. For example, wool from the shoulders and sides is usually of finest quality; next best is from the back. Around the edges of a fleece — the underbody, legs, neck — there is still good useful wool, but not as fine or long staple. This is why fleeces are carefully sorted for blending. In Ireland, recently, we were surprised to learn from the tweed weavers that a very small proportion of wool from the sheep grazing just outside in the meadows was suitable for use in their lovely fine tweeds. Much of it is too coarse for clothing fabrics, but right for carpets. All of their weaving wools are blended with wools from other countries. It is said that good wool grows on tender flesh — so good meat and fine wool come from the same spot!

Because of the self-clinging qualities of the wool fibers, it is possible to weave long-wearing fabrics from unspun wool. For this, the wool is carded or teased into long strands then laid into

9

1-15. Ross Simmons does a careful shearing job on one of his black sheep — on a handwoven blanket! (Courtesy of Paula Simmons.)

1-16. Carding machine. The bent metal teeth and the action are the same as that of hand cards. Wool is straightened and smoothed into a uniform batt, ready for spinning. (Courtesy of Paula Simmons.)

the weft. The author has used it pulled out as fine as a knitting worsted, and in strands as large around as a finger. A wonderfully lightweight but warm coverlet was woven with the spun-wool warp set at only four to the inch and a weft of bulky finger-sized unspun wool. A soft cozy poncho of fine unspun wool with a finespun wool warp set at ten to the inch has seen service for about ten years, and still looks like new.

BLACK SHEEP WOOL

Paula Simmons' black sheep handspun yarns are an elegant, luxurious addition to wool yarns for weavers and knitters. The Simmons, of Suquamish, Washington, raise their selected dark sheep and prepare the wool with experienced know-how and loving care. This results in wonderfully soft, silky yarn of superb quality in cream white through all shades of gray, warm browns, and blacks. Their yarn business is so intimate and personalized, that the color cards are coded with the names of their sheep! — from Posie's pale gray-beige to Gabriella's warm black. They are now doing an increasing amount of vegetable-dyed wool in soft, glowing colors.

1-17. Paula Simmons winding black sheep yarn onto a stick-reel (an old Colonial name for this is "Niddy Noddy"). She has just spun the wool on her modern version of the upright, castle-type wheel, a perfectly balanced wheel with ball-bearing action for high speed spinning without too much exertion. Beautifully made of hand-rubbed black walnut, by Robert Shelton of Bremerton, Washington. (Courtesy of Paula Simmons.)

1-18. Afghan, handwoven with handspun black sheep yarns. Skeins of the yarn shown are in white through grays. Spinner and weaver, Paula Simmons. (Photograph, KPEC TV, Tacoma, Washington.)

1-19. Deep soft rug woven in loop technique, using handspun yarns in many shades of natural grays and browns. Spinner and weaver, Paula Simmons. (Photograph, KPEC TV, Tacoma, Washington.)

1-20. Handspun wool, plain weave, highly textured blanket. Spinner and weaver, Paula Simmons.

11

1-21. Composition of many woven fabrics: wool, linen, cotton, silk, metallic, chenille, rayons. One way to make a decorative reference for weaves and colors. These were pinned to a framed cork bulletin board. Easy to remove, add to, or rearrange. All woven by the author. (Photograph by Kent Kammerer.)

Paula weaves beautiful afghans, woolen fabrics, and rugs from her yarns. Every process is done with care in the best possible way, including the care and feeding of their sheep so they can grow the best of wool. A series of helpful articles by Paula Simmons in the *Handweaver and Craftsman Magazine* is well worth looking for. In this series, packed with information, she shares the results of her years of spinning, weaving, and working with her black sheep wool.

1-22. Twill weave, wool coating fabric. Woven by the author. (Photograph by Kent Kammerer.)

1-23. Alpaca yarn. Woven in Peru. Brushed surface on plain weave tapestry. Collection of Betsey Bess. (Photograph by Kent Kammerer.)

COTTON

Cotton, too, like animal fibers, is made up of different length fibers, but cotton fibers are only about three-eighths of an inch to two-and-one-half inches long and these must be mixed and blended. Thousands of years ago some very observant early-day man must have noticed that the natural movement of the cotton fibers was all in one direction. He took advantage of this and reinforced the natural direction by twisting or spinning. Like linen, cotton yarn has more strength when wet.

Left
1-24. Plain weave cotton placemat. Woven by the author. (Photograph by Kent Kammerer.)

Below left
1-25. Open weave drapery fabric, cotton nub yarn and fine bouclé wound together on one shuttle. Woven by the author. (Photograph by Kent Kammerer.)

Below right
1-26. Velvety cotton chenille on coarse and fine cotton warp. Woven by author. (Photograph by Kent Kammerer.)

Linen is a bast fiber from the stem of the flax plant. Fibers from the intermediate layer, between the outside bark and the woody core, are as long as the plant is tall, up to 20 inches or more.

A flax field in full bloom is a beautiful sight, knee high, with soft green leaves topped by small bright blue flowers. It took a great deal of vision and ingenuity to convert this stalky plant into strands of fiber that could be spun into one of the most durable and luxurious of yarns. Probably the first vegetable fiber known to man, linen was processed and used in earliest recorded Egyptian times. Flax grew in the Nile Valley, and perhaps the qualities of flax fiber were first observed when the Nile overflowed, soaking and breaking apart the woody stems, revealing the fibers — retting, or soaking, is one of the first steps in releasing the fiber from the stems. The hardy pioneer spirit must have been taxed to the limit, working with these bast fibers. They are resistant, tough, not easily dyed, spun, or woven!

1-27. Linen casement cloth of bleached and natural linen. Weaver, Lewis Mayhew. (Photograph, Audio-Visual Services, University of Washington.)

1-28. Light and darker gray-green linen. Canvas weave upholstery. Weaver, Clara Chapman. (Photograph by Kent Kammerer.)

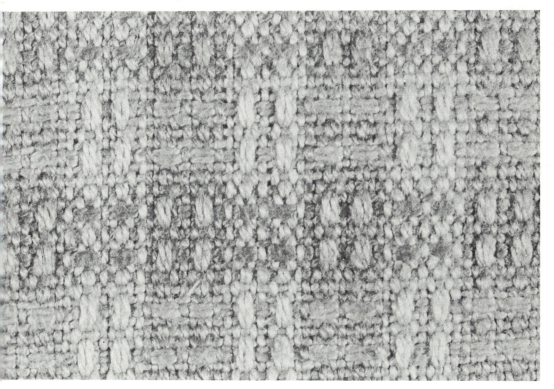

SILK AND SERICULTURE

Raising of silkworms and producing raw silk

The romance of silk reads like the most breathtaking of thrillers. China's closely guarded secret of sericulture and silk weaving, practiced from remote times, was kept her own for over three thousand years. Many legends and fables are told. When these gorgeous woven silks were first brought out of China, plots and counter-plots were devised to learn the secret of how and where the lovely fibers were made. As a result, the dangerous but profitable six-thousand-mile "Silk Road" was opened about 126 B.C. and silks were carried by caravan to Persia, Arabia, and Syria. About A.D. 550, the Byzantine Emperor Justinian persuaded two Persian monks to smuggle silkworms and mulberry-tree seeds in their hollow bamboo staffs, and in this way silk culture was finally introduced into Europe.

An attempt at sericulture was begun in Mexico about 1531; about 1619, King James I sent silkworms to Virginia. By the middle of the eighteenth century enough silk was being made in the American Colonies to export more than ten thousand pounds of high quality yarn from Georgia to England, but it was not until the nineteenth century that a real attempt was made to create a home industry of silk production. High costs of manufacture, however, prevented it from becoming a major industry, and it was replaced by cotton.

1-29. Silk. Shiny, extremely fine, woven into a detailed flower and water pattern. A "fingernail" weave. Each fingernail of the weaver is filed to a tiny saw-tooth edge and they are then used as beaters to push the very fine threads into place, creating this lovely brocade pattern. Woven in Japan. Collection of the author. (Photograph by Kent Kammerer.)

1-30. Silk. Raw silk and nub spun silk, with some inlays of unspun wool. Woven by the author. (Photograph by Kent Kammerer.)

Shipwrecks, spies, rewards, bounties, elaborate smuggling plots, and silk-worker immigrants from Japan were involved in the spreading knowledge of and desire for the "Queen of the Fibers" — and it all started with the product of a little silkworm!

A WEAVERS' GUILD SILK PROJECT

Learning about silk production
— a good classroom project

I still remember the thrill and wonder of having a turn at reeling silk from a cocoon, at a very early age in school. Silkworms are easily contained in trays and the moths do not fly, so the project is manageable as well as fascinating. At the 1968 Santa Clara County Fair, the Glenna Harris Guild of weavers in San Jose, California, set up a very worthwhile educational exhibit on silk and sericulture. This thorough — and thoroughly interested — group was sparked by Mrs. Fumiko Pentler, who had worked with silkworms as a child on her grandmother's farm in Japan. For the demonstration and exhibit at the Fair, these weavers all learned the procedures; they imported pounds of cocoons so they could show the reeling of silk and also let the children try.

Since it was related to local history, pioneer silk production having been started in California at San Jose, the interest and participation was exceptional. The Guild continued by installing a silk exhibit in the Cupertino Public Library, and a live silkworm exhibit is being planned for a museum. This group of weavers has contributed a great deal to the understanding of other natural fibers, too. From 1964 on they have explored, studied, and prepared exhibits and demonstrations of weaving with plant fibers, step-by-step displays with photographs of plant fibers, including the plants and seeds. Another comprehensive exhibit and weaving demonstration deals with animal fibers, and there is one on man-made fibers.

All this represents a great and very complete educational effort. Mrs. Pentler's account of the Glenna Harris Guild activities, published in the Winter, 1969, issue of *Handweaver and Craftsman Magazine*, contains information on sericulture and a very good reference list for future study. Addresses for information on where to obtain silkworms and cocoons are included.

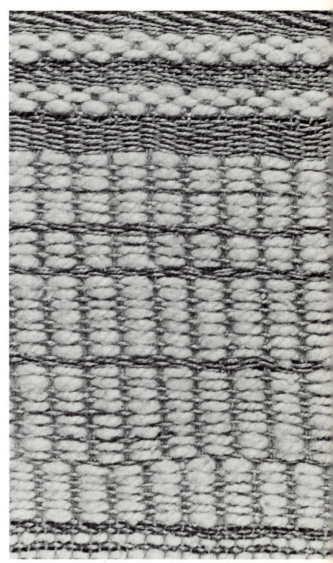

1-31. Heavy raw silk on linen warp, bedspread fabric. Woven by the author. (Photograph by Kent Kammerer.)

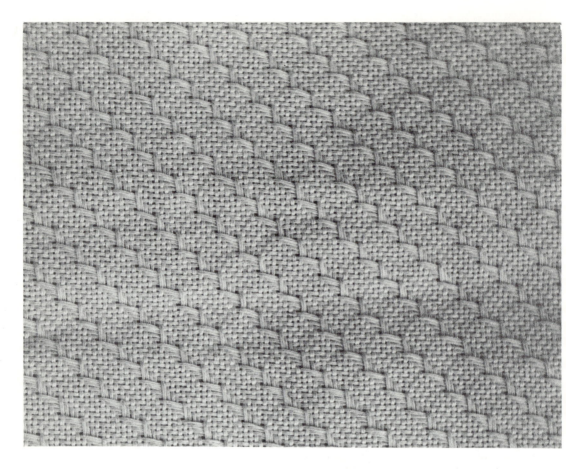

1-32, 33. Two textiles woven with ramie yarns. Weaver, Russell E. Groff. Ramie yarns in a selection of colors and sizes are available from Robin and Russ Handweavers, 533 N. Adams St., McMinnville, Oregon, 97128.

RAMIE

Cloth woven of this fiber looks and acts much like linen. It is absorbent, strong, and versatile. Such varied textiles as a sheer so fine that it can be drawn through a ring to men's wear suitings, other clothing fabrics, towelling, and household textiles are woven from ramie yarn.

OTHER WOOL-BEARING ANIMALS

Llama, alpaca, and vicuña

These South American animals, distant relatives of the camel, produce an exceptionally soft and luxurious fiber with natural colors so varied and lovely that the yarn is rarely dyed. Colors range from a cream-white through yellow-browns to dark browns and black. These yarns are easily brushed into a fluffy nap after weaving, as the wool consists of long fibers and fine silky hairs.

Llamas are beasts of burden, able to carry up to about one-hundred-pound loads. They have long necks and spiky dispositions! Their coats are multi-colored, in combinations of white, golden brown, and black. The hair is coarser and shorter than that of the alpaca.

Alpacas are smaller than llamas and have quite heavy coats. The yarn resembles mohair, but is not quite as strong.

Alpaca and llamas are found in Peru and Bolivia in the high Andes, and have been domesticated by the Indians of the region.

The vicuña, an elusive little creature, bears the finest, softest wool of all, a light brown. It is very scarce and very expensive, because unfortunately the vicuña must be hunted, killed, and skinned, to obtain the wool.

Camel

Camel hair is in great demand for fine wool textiles, and the supply is limited. The hairy coat, a mixture of fine down about two-and-a-half inches long and coarse outer hairs, grows in heavy layers with exceptional insulating qualities, which are retained in the yarn. At certain seasons, when the camel sheds quantities of the down and hair, the fibers are harvested and blended, much like wool, for a suitable fiber to spin into yarn. Its natural color is the familiar pleasant medium-light brown. The yarn is soft and has a fine nap. Sometimes it is blended with sheep wool.

Goats

Several kinds of goats contribute fibers to the textile industry. Two familiar ones are mohair and cashmere. These fibers have excellent qualities and are usually blended with sheep wool or other fibers for the best yarn. The hair is shed or obtained by combing. Goat hair is more lustrous and elastic than wool and makes a fabric that wrinkles less than most others; its natural colors are white and brown but it takes and retains brilliant dyed colors.

Mohair comes from the Angora goat. The fibers are long and curly, measuring about nine to twelve inches. Kid mohair, from young goats, is the finest and best.

Cashmere, from Tibetan goats, is a luxury fiber like vicuña, long fibered and glossy with a soft wool down underlayer. It is shed, or combed from the animal, and usually mixed with wool. The yield is quite small, so it is expensive. Cashmere yarn is exceptionally good at holding its shape when woven or knit.

Angora rabbit

This unbelievably fluffy, soft creature is not to be confused with the Angora goat! It's hair — white, long, light, and smooth — is obtained by combing and is spun into cloud-soft yarn. Sometimes it is blended with wool to make a yarn with a little more body, but still soft and with a furry texture.

Dogs

Many breeds of long-haired dogs provide hair for spinning into yarn — either blended with wool or spun alone. Poodles, Samoyedes, collies — almost any longhair whose healthy coat produces combings can provide fiber for spinning.

OTHER ANIMAL FIBERS

Horsehair

Coarse, smooth, and bristly, horsehair has limited use as yarn. It is used in haircloth, the scratchy, stiff cloth used by tailors to stiffen collars, and to some extent is still used in mattresses. I have seen it used in bunches as weft in a rug, or a few stiff ends of it in a 3-D weaving.

Cowhair

In Scandinavian countries this is spun with wool. The yarn is excellent for rugs. The dark hairs are attractive in the yarn and add a slightly hairy texture to the weave.

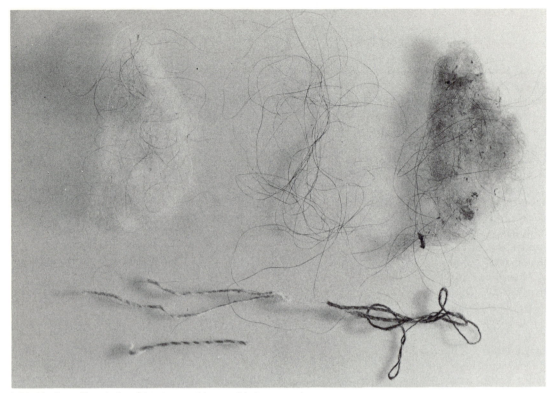

1-34. Musk ox fiber. Left, white down with guard hairs, two ply handspun yarn. Center, long guard hairs. Right, light grey down with guard hairs, single ply handspun grey yarn. Courtesy of Mrs. Richard Field, spinner and weaver. (Photograph by Kent Kammerer.)

1-35. A musk ox family at the University of Alaska. (Photograph by Jimmy Bedford.)

Musk Ox

The musk ox, that little known creature, is now being bred in Alaska for crops of hair or wool for spinning. Beneath the long, shiny guard hairs grows soft, downy wool which can be spun with no preparation other than removing the few guard hairs caught in it. It is gossamer — so soft you can scarcely feel it — but it spins readily into finest yarn, even finer than cashmere. Pale gray and off-white in color, this lovely fiber shows promise of being a contribution to luxury yarns. It is very expensive at this time, but production is increasing. The Eskimo word for the wool is "qiviut," meaning "under-wool."

Musk oxen were almost lost to us. In the past, they were hunted until only a few thousand remained, a small band that had been stranded behind a barricade of ice in Northeastern Canada and Greenland during the Ice Age, which protected them from the Eskimo hunters. Centuries ago, Arctic adventurers were no doubt amazed to see small clouds of airy wool blowing and settling on the tundra. As time went on, measures were taken to save the species and in 1954 domestication began with seven calves taken from the Thelon Game Sanctuary. In just a few days, they were gentled and seemed eager to establish friendly relations with their captors.

After ten years of thorough research and care, these appealing beasts are established at the University of Alaska, in Fort Chimo, Quebec, Canada, and Bardu, Norway. Their beautiful, downy wool is being spun and Eskimos are knitting it into luxury garments. Remarkably warm and light lacy scarves are being created. Each village uses its own distinctive designs taken from ancient carvings.

OTHER NATURAL FIBERS

Without getting too botanical, we have sorted out some of the more familiar names of fibers and plants. There are hundreds of different plants producing useful bast and structural fibers.

Bast fiber: This comes from the inner layer of a plant stem, such as flax.

Structural fiber: This comes from long, fleshy leaves of plants, such as pineapple.

These fibers, most of which are quite stiff and require breaking down and softening, are usually not spun in the sense that animal fibers are. They

1-37. Sea grass. Note where strips have been knotted together. This makes a pleasant change in texture in the plain weave.

1-36. Raffia. Natural color on a finer dark green warp.

1-38. Abaca. Smooth and quite flexible.

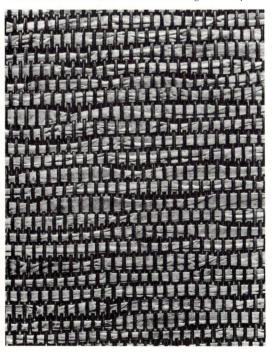

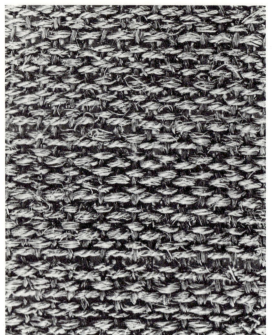

1-39. Ixtle. Harsh, stiff fiber from Mexico. Much like sisal.

1-40. Sisal. Fibers are slightly twisted to make a rope-like yarn. Very prickly and independent.

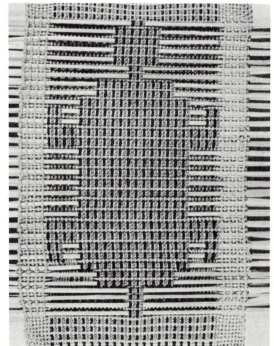

1-41. Jute. Burlap, the same as gunny sacking. (Above group, photographed by Kent Kammerer.)

1-42. Matchstick size bamboo strips, cotton warp and weft, combined with a special weave to create a turtle design. Design and method, Mary Pendleton. Weaver, Lila Winn. (Photograph by William Eng.)

are twisted or rolled into flexible weft material, or used in straight lengths. Cordage (ropes, lines, cords, twine), burlap sacks, mats, rugs, rug backings, and so on, are made from these plant fibers.

Hemp: A plant native to Asia, but grown in many other countries.

Sisal: From the agave plant. The fiber is similar to hemp.

Manila hemp: Not a true hemp, but very much like it. Taken from the abaca plant.

Abaca cloth: A crisp, fairly fine cloth made from abaca plant fiber.

Jute: A plant whose fibers are used in burlap or gunny (gunny-sacks).

Coir: Stiff, harsh fiber from the shell of cocoanuts. Coco door mats are made from this material. It is also twisted into cord and woven into rugs.

Piña: Fiber from pineapple leaves, used for sheer, fine cloth and slightly coarser mats made in the Philippines.

Leaves, stems, mosses, and *branches* are also used for weaving just about as they are gathered. The tough, strong ones become structural, and then we have arrived at basket weaving.

Figures 1-36 — 1-42 show placemats woven of plant fibers.

MIXTURES AND ODD LOTS

Cottolin. Cotton and linen are combined in a yarn called cottolin. Spun and used in Sweden. The yarn is available to weavers in a selection of colors and in three or four sizes. It has the handsomeness of linen, but a cottolin fabric does not wrinkle as much as pure linen.

Viyella. Lambswool and cotton spun together to make a very soft, fine yarn that is shrinkproof and washable when woven into fabric or made into socks. Made in England.

Other combinations are spun together in various proportions to make yarns: rayon and cotton, rayon and jute, and so on. Usually the combined fibers make a yarn with the best qualities of each. Cotton-and-linen has the sheen and durability of linen, softened a bit by the cotton. In rayon-and-jute combination, the rayon adds strength and luster, the jute contributes its own rough texture, toned down.

Fashion fabrics often have new combinations of fibers and new spins, such as mink hairs carded into wool for a slightly hairy texture; metallic thread twisted into cotton, silk, or wool yarns; mohair loops in fine, smooth wool.

Random colored nubs of wool in the yarn are usually associated with tweeds. At Kilcar, County Donegal, Ireland, at a large tweed weaving factory where they also spin and dye their own yarns, we saw how this was done. Odd bits of short fleece left from carding and sorting are dyed in many colors, in separate dye lots. The textile designer decides what color nubs he wants in the yarn for a certain fabric, figures out about how often he wants them repeated, and in what proportion, if more than one color is to be used. The wool bits are let into a huge cage-like drum, floor to ceiling high, with plain wool ready for spinning. The wool is forcefully blown about until well mixed, then it is blown through a pipe to the spinning room on another floor, where it is spun into the well-known tweed yarn with scattered dots of color throughout.

METALS, METALLIC YARN

Pure gold and silver threads are often incorporated to highlight and beautify the finest woven works of art. They combine especially well with silk, adding richness and luster.

Metallic yarns are made of metals or synthetic materials. They add glitter and accent. Some are spun on a silk or rayon core, others are twisted into cotton or silk yarn. Some are flat and smooth, others are spun. Their most practical use is as an added accent and not as the principal yarn in fabric construction.

PLASTIC STRIPS

Plastmattor, a product of Sweden, is the name given to strips of plastic made for weaving into soft, durable, practical rugs and mats. Woven on a nylon warp, these rugs are completely washable. The strips come in two widths, wound on spools. The material is translucent, a bit heavier than the plastic used for food bags, and comes in several soft colors.

MAN-MADE FIBERS

We are living in an exciting age of great experimentation and progress in the creation and use of man-made materials. Synthetic yarns and fibers are spinning out of test tubes and laboratories so fast that it is almost impossible to keep an up to date list. As the years go by, the production and use of natural fibers will no doubt continue to diminish. To some extent this has already happened to silk, linen, and wool.

Synthetic yarns have their place, certainly. They make possible the drip-dry washables, the wear-forever textiles. The first man-made fibers met with deep-seated prejudice and disdain by the natural-fiber manufacturers and users. Strange, made-up names were coined to relate these new fibers to the known ones, for example, rayon was originally called "Artificial Silk." Trying to improve the image, this was soon reduced to "A. Silk" in advertising, and even "Klis" — silk spelled backwards!

As newer laboratory and factory techniques improved the yarns, they came to have their own place in the textile world. Some are pretty good imitations of natural fibers, but many of them have taken on their own identity and are frankly fake, filling special requirements. Now they are generally accepted for what they are. When it was realized, in the early 1920's, that trying so hard to imitate silk and other natural fibers was not very acceptable, a whole new approach to the making of synthetic fibers opened up.

GENERIC NAMES

Some of the most widely-known names of man-made yarns and textiles are rayon, nylon, acrylic, acetate, glass. These and others are generic — or family — names, like wool, cotton, and so on.

Trade names are legion. Although composed of combinations of chemicals and other substance, some of these yarns resemble natural fibers, while others have a characteristic look, feel, and smell of their own. More and more are becoming available to the handweaver. The manufacturing procedures are much too technical to go into in this book; our intention here is only to make you aware of them, and for this reason we have included photographs of some of the yarns and textiles woven with them (Figures 1-43 — 1-47). For those interested in more information we have

Above: 1-43. Wall-hanging of black rayon straw. Weaver, Katherine Strohecker. (Photograph, Audio-Visual Services, University of Washington.)

Below: 1-44. Rayon straw placemat. Smooth, pliable, washable. (Photograph by Kent Kammerer.)

Left above: 1-45. Saran, polyester, and acrylic yarns. Top, open weave of yarn composed of many fine fibers loosely spun. Bottom, close weave, smooth flexible extruded plastic. *Left below:* 1-46. Synthetic straw yarn made of fine soft fibers, loosely spun. Woven on cotton warp. *Above:* 1-47. Rayon and jute spun together for weft. Cotton warp. Woven by the author. (Photographs by Kent Kammerer.)

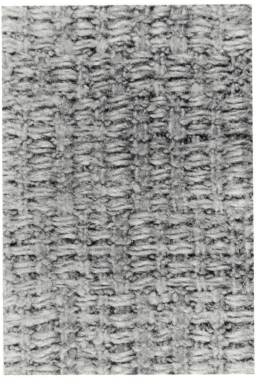

given sources in the "List of Useful Reference Publications" on page 138.

Just as each kind of yarn has its own personality, cloth woven from each is distinctive. The most noticeable difference will be in looks, then in the feel, or "hand." Cloth woven of soft wool, smoothly spun, feels and looks different from a mat woven of jute, a harsh, stiff fiber. You choose the yarn to fit the project. Yardage for a suit is woven with good quality wool, firmly spun, pleasant to touch, resilient. Carpet wool must be long-wearing and good quality, but does not have to be as soft to the touch as wearable wool. Cotton yarn for household goods, like bedsheets, must be very strong and fine to withstand factory finishing for washability, wear, looks, and long use. A handweaver must use good judgment in choice of yarn for any weaving. Most of us, I am sure, have had the unhappy experience of weaving something beautiful, but totally unsuited to the purpose. One of my mistakes was weaving a double-face fabric of leather strips and wool for a jacket — only to find that it was too stiff to wear comfortably! The pillows made from it were great! Another clothing fabric made from a lovely fine wool was too scratchy against the skin, but worked well when it was made into a lined skirt. So do think through your weaving projects — from yarn to finish.

1-48. Sheep.

Sheep. Once a year the heavy coat is shorn from the sheep, although in some countries the sheep grow so much wool that it can be clipped more often. The usual crop, however, is just one fleece from each sheep each year.

Shearing. The wool is cut from the sheep so it comes off in one mat-like piece. This is done with special shears by experienced shearers who do it very quickly and neatly. When released by the shearer, after losing the heavy coat, which may weigh anywhere from about five to fifteen pounds, the sheep feel so light and airy that they skip and leap about like lambs. They do look a little peeled and forlorn, but the wool begins growing back quite fast, just as your hair does after a haircut. (See figure 1-15.)

1-49. Shearing.

Fleece. Each fleece is folded in a certain way, carefully kept in one piece easy to unfold for sorting, and tied into a bundle with twine or ends of the fleece. The bundles are then put into enormous burlap bags standing about eight feet high. These huge sacks of wool are shipped to the wool markets to be sorted and sold.

Carding. To clean it, the wool is "teased", then carded. Teasing is pulling and shaking the wool to open it out and remove stems, leaves, straw, and even old dried bumblebees caught in the sheep's coat. Carding further cleans, but its main purpose is to straighten the fibers in preparation for spinning. Hand carding is done with two paddle-like tools with rows of bent wires like multiple small bent fingertips. These wires do the same job fingers do in teasing wool. When a fleece is comparatively clean the preliminary step of teasing may be all that is necessary.

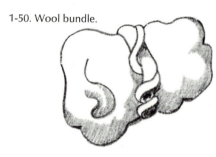

1-50. Wool bundle.

In carding, a bit of wool is put on one card, then the cards are dragged across each other in opposite directions, pulling out and combing the wool fibers. After this the wool is shaped into a long, narrow fluffy cylinder called a sliver or rolag, and is ready for spinning. Done by hand, this is a time-consuming process. In industry, huge high-speed machines are used to do the same thing rapidly on a large scale. There are also small home-size mechanical carders with a toothed surface drum that can be rotated by hand or a small motor to speed up the process. (See figure 1-16.)

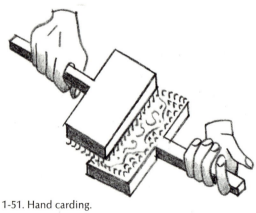

1-51. Hand carding.

1-52. Hand spinning.

1-53. Spinning wheel.

Spinning. To create long strands of material strong enough to weave with, the fibers, which are all of different lengths, must be twisted together. Wool fiber is constructed as a series of overlapping scales, like shingles, so the fiber will cling to itself. Originally wool was spun by twisting it by hand, rolling it along the thigh. Then a drop spindle was devised, a simple wooden tool that twists the fibers as it is turned or dropped, spinning like a top. Later, spinning wheels were developed to do the twisting with the help of a wheel and foot pedal. Finally machinery was invented to spin fibers on a grand scale, with rows and rows of spools filling with spun yarns all at once. (See figure 1-17 for another type of spinning wheel.)

Wool fiber, magnified. The sketch shows clearly how the overlapping shingle-like layers create little hooks that grasp each other.

1-54. Wool fiber.

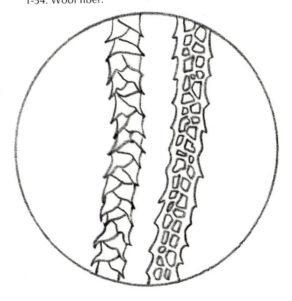

1-55. Cotton plant.   1-56 Cotton boll.

Cotton plant. The cotton plant is a shrub about three to five feet tall, with yellow or white flowers. When the flowers go to seed, they become cotton bolls. Cotton fiber is really seed hair. The seeds are encased in a round pod with a rough, hard covering. When the seed pod bursts open, revealing a puff of white, the cotton is ready to be harvested. A cotton field ready for harvest looks a little as though a light fluffy snow had fallen, forming hundreds of separate snowballs.

Picking Cotton. Before the invention of the mechanized cotton picker cotton had to be picked by hand, a hard tedious labor often requiring hundreds of field hands for a large crop — men, women, and children. Now big machines pass over the cotton plants, plucking off the ripe bolls. Not as picturesque, but faster!

1-57. Picking cotton.

Cleaning, baling, and spinning. The cotton must be cleaned of seeds, leaves, and stems, but since there is no natural oil in the fiber washing is not necessary. The oil is in the small seeds, and cottonseed oil is another valuable product of this plant. The cotton is packed in large bales, wrapped in burlap and bound, ready for shipment to spinning mills. The spinning process is very much like that of wool spinning, with variations required by the different characteristics of the cotton fibers. There are no convenient little hooked scales such as those in wool fiber; on the contrary, cotton fibers have a very smooth surface. Luxury cotton is still spun by hand, on a spinning wheel or small spindle. Like linen, cotton is so strong when spun that it can be made into incredibly fine, strong sewing thread. Unlike wool, which can be spun on a drop spindle, a cotton spindle must rest on a smooth surface to avoid breakage of the tender fibers.

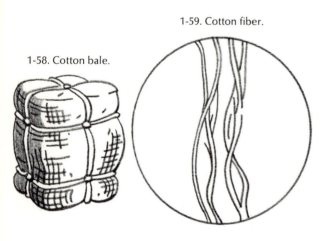

1-59. Cotton fiber.

1-58. Cotton bale.

Cotton fiber, magnified. Magnified under a microscope, cotton fiber has the appearance of a lazily twisting ribbon or flattened tube.

Preparation for spinning

The first step in the factory cleaning process is ginning — removing the seeds from the lint. In most varieties of cotton the seeds will still retain a coating of down and so they go through another process called delinting. The product of this is called linters — fibers too short to spin, but that have many uses including use for absorbent cotton, felt, and for mixtures with wool.

The cleaned cotton is pressed into large bales. A bale may contain the fiber from several acres of cotton plants. Each process has its own terms:

Terms for successive steps in mixing and preparing the material for spinning are descriptive, and as many steps as needed are used to refine the cotton for various grades of yarn.

Picking or opening. This is the same as teasing wool, resulting in a roll of fiber.

Carding. The result is a sliver, which is a thin fluffy strip of fiber.

Combing. Used in preparing the very finest yarns, this step results in slivers of smaller size.

Drawing. Makes even smaller slivers.

Slubbing. A slight twist for strength is put into the slivers, which are now quite thin and fragile.

Intermediate slubbing results in a twisted sliver wound on a bobbin.

Roving: The refined cotton is now ready for spinning, and is wound on a bobbin. The large rug cotton yarn available to weavers is called roving. It is a loosely spun, soft yarn, as thick as a pencil and comparatively inexpensive.

Hand preparation is essentially the same as the factory procedure with the yarn-maker working the cotton until it is straight and clean and ready to be spun.

After spinning, the yarn is dyed in skeins. Then it is wound on spools or cones, or put up in skeins of various sizes.

Mercerized cotton

Mercerized cotton has more sheen than untreated cotton. This is due to a chemical process that not only makes the yarn more lustrous but also makes it stronger, colorfast, and more receptive to dyes. In addition, the treated fibers are easier to process because they become rounder and more co-operative.

FLAX INTO THREAD

While in Belfast, Ireland, recently, it seemed appropriate to go to the very old Linen Library there to read up on this product, which has been and is such an important industry in Ireland. An old book explained at length the many procedures necessary to break this stubborn material down for spinning into a suitable weaving yarn. The necessary processes are essentially the same whether done by hand or modern machinery. From the Linen Library, then, here is an account of the steps taken by a long-ago farmer to convert his crop of flax into fibers for spinning and weaving.

Preparation of flax for spinning

The slender flax plant must be pulled at just the right moment, when it is about two-thirds yellow and the seeds are tinged with brown. Bundles of the plants are tied and stacked like sheaves of grain. There are many long steps and much handling between the harvesting of the plants and a spool of fine linen thread. As is true with any procedure, the language is its own, often quite descriptive.

Rippling. The tops of the plant are drawn through a "ripple," which is like a large comb. The seeds are thriftily caught in a sheet, to be used in products like linseed oil, or fed to cattle and horses.

The stems are tied into stooks or sheaves, stacked, and allowed to air thoroughly and dry for a few days.

1-60. Flax plant.

Retting. The purpose of this important step is to soak the fibers and let them ferment in order to break them down enough to separate. The process takes two or three weeks. Bundles are weighted with stones or sod and placed in water; picturesquely, this is done in quiet ponds or rivers. Sometimes crate-like containers or woven wicker frames were made to hold the bundles upright, tightly packed. Retting is complete when the fiber breaks away freely from the woody outside part. The long fibers are then cleaned, drained, and spread to dry.

Grassing. The bundles of fibers are arranged in straight rows on a grassy area and may lie there for a month or more; in some places they are exposed to dew and rain for several months. The amount of exposure, time, and care, makes a difference in the color, which can vary from ivory to dark gray-tan.

Rollers. The fibers are then run through rollers to further break and clean them.

Flax break. A device with a series of long bars and a beater to break down the woody parts still more. These drop out, leaving the fibers.

On to the scutching mill for more beating

Hackle. This is a block of long, strong metal teeth for further cleaning out all straw and woody particles. The fibers are run through this, as through a comb, and then they finally begin to look like a fiber related to yarn. Long fibers are called the line — short fibers, the tow.

During the scutching process, short fibers, called "scutching tow," fall out. These are salvaged and used for coarse cloths and slubby yarns.

After these soakings, beatings and combings, the farmer has a product that can be sent to the spinning mills. If he wants to have his flax spun by hand, a few more steps must be taken to prepare it.

Roughing. Separating the fibers still more. They can be separated many times until they are mere hairs — and still take it! More hackling disentangles and further cleans and combs the fibers, separating line from tow. After more sorting, combing, and cleaning, the line (long fibers) is beautifully smooth and glossy.

Spinning is done with either wet or dry fibers. Wet spinning produces a strong, tightly twisted yarn, not quite as silky looking as the dry spun,

1-61. Hackling flax.

but a good, durable yarn. Wet-spinning yarn must be carefully and quickly dried to prevent mold. Hanks of spun yarn can be bleached, half bleached, or just boiled and left the natural gray-tan linen color.

The tow and other waste, such as broken ends, can be carded and combed into a roving, which is then spun like the long line fibers.

Linen yardage

After the linen yarns have been woven into yardage, crofting or grass bleaching is a picturesque part of the process. Long lengths of linen fabric woven in factories are stretched out on the linen bleaching greens — flat grassy plots reserved for this. Several hundred yards are stitched together, end to end, then laid out row upon row, to bleach in the dew and sun. When white enough, the textile is blued, starched, dried, beetled (more pounding to give it luster), calendered (heat with pressure), and then — finally — the yardage is ready for market, to be made into table linens, towels, and such. An amazingly violent series of procedures, but it produces magnificent linens of extreme durability and beauty.

Hand weaving with linen

Linen yarns, even after the soaking, pounding, carding, and spinning, are still tough, and usually have to be moistened when hand woven. This un-yielding quality of linen is one of the reasons it is so very useful in table linens and upholstery materials. It will withstand a lot of wear and washing. It must be treated in a special way to become absorbent enough for towels and refined enough for clothing. American pioneers wove a fabric called linsey-woolsy, for clothing. This material had a linen warp with a wool weft. I'm sure the soft wool helped to make the scratchy linen feel a little easier on those pioneer necks.

Flax fiber, magnified. Much enlarged, the flax fiber shows joints or nodules, much like bamboo. It tapers to a point, the surface is smooth.

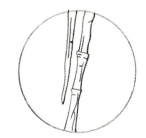

1-62. Flax fiber.

COCOONS INTO SILK

The destiny of a silkworm is to become a butterfly, but first he must surround himself with a cocoon. He spins miles of fine silk to create his protective casing, but in sericulture he is not allowed to emerge because this would break the delicate strands he has spun.

The silkworm

Tiny new worms feast greedily on mulberry leaves; as they live and grow on trays of leaves (figure 1-63), their steady munching sounds like falling rain. Within 30 days they will start to spin their cocoons, and in about two or three days each silkworm will spin a thousand yards of continuous silk filament. Ten days later the worm has changed from pupa to moth, and is ready to make a hole in his silken home and emerge to try his wings. Now the timing must be watched very carefully. If the chrysalis does break out, the threads will be torn. Before this can happen, the cocoons are plunged into water and boiled to release the fibers. This done, filament ends of several cocoons are attached to a reel and strands of silk are reeled off as the cocoons bob in the warm water. This reeled silk is too delicate for all but the sheerest fabric, so a throwing process is used to double and twist the fiber into different sizes of thread. These threads are then stretched to make them smooth and even, and washed to remove all traces of gum. They can then be bleached, dyed, and woven. As a rule, very long lengths are reeled off the cocoon, but broken lengths, waste, and unreelable parts are salvaged and also spun.

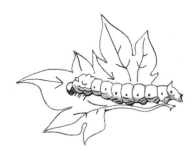

1-63. Silk worm.

1-64. Cocoon, chrysalis.

1-65. Reeling silk.

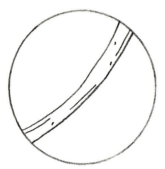

1-66. Silk filament.

1-67. Wild silk filament.

1-68. Ramie plant.

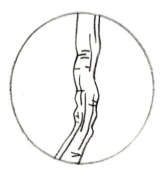

1-69. Ramie fiber.

Wild silk

Wild silk, which is rough and unevenly spun, is taken from cocoons found in trees; wild silk-worms feed on whatever leaves are available. The cocoons are usually gathered after the moth has emerged, so the filament lengths are short, resulting in a rougher spin. This silk, also called raw silk, is very strong. Its natural color is a light brown, and it cannot be bleached. Although rather rough and dull, wild silk has a great beauty of its own. Pongee and Tussar cloth are woven from wild silk.

Silk filament, magnified. As shown, silk filament is smooth and straight without much surface texture, compared to wool. Raw silk, or wild silk, is curving and ribbon-like with more roughness on the surface.

RAMIE PLANT

Ramie was grown and used in ancient China and Japan, it was known in India, is grown in Florida, and will grow in almost any warm, moist climate. A shrub of the nettle family, it grows tall, resembling the sunflower. The fibers are released from the stalk in much the same way that linen is taken from the flax plant stem. Since it is also a bast fiber, it must be soaked, dried, combed, drawn, spun, and a gummy substance must also be carefully and completely removed to obtain the very white, silky fibers. Unspun ramie is feather-soft and looks so delicate it is hard to believe its strength, when spun, but it makes an extremely strong thread and can be very finely spun. Ceremonial draperies of ramie cloth, probably over three thousand years old, have been discovered in the tombs of the Pharaohs in Egypt.

BASKET WEAVING USING
NATURAL MATERIALS

Basket weaving is an important part of the whole handweaving picture, so in the chapter that follows we relate it to textile weaving.

Pencil sketches for figures 1-48 — 69 by Mary Bassetti.

From source to woven baskets

Baskets are woven, too — much like cloth. The upright ribs are the warp. The flexible, horizontal fibers are the weft. Proof that some of the earliest weaving was the interlacement of branches for a windscreen or shelter wall is in our photograph of the protecting fence in a re-creation of an Iron Age habitation, outside Copenhagen, Denmark, shown on Color Page 84.

Crafts are a bridge to the past, letting us see and learn much about the people who went before us. Baskets were an important part of the daily life and craftsmanship of people all over the world; a serious student of basketry can identify the exact people, place, climate, and way of life from the basket materials, shapes, designs, and methods of construction used. Shapes are as varied as the materials. Originated by primitive people, baskets were made as useful objects, needed for a real reason, and constructed from materials at hand. This, in turn, dictated the sizes, shapes, and manner of construction. From a carefully woven cradle for a midwest Indian papoose to an open-weave but strong basket made to gather clams or camas roots by Northwest Indians, or a splint wood two-decker New England pie basket — each kind was a practical item made of material growing nearby. Study of basketry reveals impressive evidence of the ingenuity of man; given a need and materials to devise an object, he has the ability to make it beautiful and right.

BASKETS AND TEXTILES

The craft of basket weaving is a forerunner of textile weaving. The two are closely related — first cousins, if not brothers. The differences are in the exact methods used. A loom is not necessary for basket weaving because of the rigid strength of the stakes or warp. They do not need to be stretched and fastened in tension. Baskets of pli-able material are usually started or woven completely over a form to keep the desired shape.

A study of woven basket patterns is interesting to a weaver for ideas on different ways to weave. After all, one of our basic cloth weaves, called "basket weave," was undoubtedly taken from that source. Classically, the weave is over and under two warps with two wefts in the same shed. In practice, though, many are woven with one and one or two and one, or other variations. The double weft is often replaced by a very wide single one, which gives the effect of double weft over two warps at a time. Baskets, being a three-dimensional form of weaving, must be structurally sound for their purpose as containers.

Our heritage of woven baskets and mats from the American Indians and primitives throughout the world is a fascinating study of design for use, and use of material at hand. Some — created as works of art — were so carefully made that they have lasted hundreds of years for us to see and learn the methods of construction. Others were put together quickly, used and discarded, much as we use paper goods today. Containers for foods were fashioned from growing things; the Pacific Northwest Indians wove baskets so tight they were

2-1. Basket weave. Two wefts over two warps. Drawing by Micheal Moshier.

used for food-boiling pots. Hot stones in the water heated it. These people also wove rain hats and capes from the inside of cedar bark and cattail leaves. Many Indians wove baby cradles and arrow holders. Food was harvested and stored in baskets. Clothing, floor and wall mats, hats and trays — all were made from indigenous materials for a particular need. Basketry material is as universal and varied as the geography and the peoples who use the material.

PATTERN AND DESIGN

Patterns are woven in. These may be of different colors or kinds of weft material. A naturally light or black material may be used to contrast with a natural red-brown, or some fibers may be dyed in bright colors. One basket from the Yukon has bits of blue wool fabric woven in for a touch of color. Another way to create a design or a change in texture in a one-color article is in the weave, for example, a plain weave and a twill, twining in alternating directions, spots of pattern woven in with a coarser or doubled weft heavier than the background.

MATERIALS

A partial list of materials suitable for baskets will give you some ideas:
• Raffia. This versatile material consists of fibers obtained from the leaves of a species of palm tree. It can be woven, crocheted, used to embroider, braided, or knotted. Tough, but very pliable, it can be split lengthwise into quite fine strips. Available at most craft material suppliers.
• Rattan and cane. Reed, one of the most commonly used and familiar basket materials, is obtained from the cane or rattan palm. This palm has long, unbranched, jointed stems that grow to a height of several hundred feet, attaching themselves to surrounding trees or shrubs. The tough outside layer is used for seating-cane and furniture, split or whole. Reeds are made from the inside of the stem.
• Willow. Polished willow twigs are a common and very satisfactory basket material. Splints are made from the stems.
• Corn husks. The husks are flexible and provide a variety of soft natural colors, especially the inner

husks. Selected colors are often used for overlay ornamentation. Mats, bags, and dolls are made with the dried leaves.
• Cattail, bullrush, tule. Both the leaves and stems of these are useful. The stems are straight, very strong, smooth, and polished; the long pliable leaves can be braided or folded.
• Sweet grass. Soft, gray-green, delicately scented, this grass makes a fine weft. It is sometimes used as trim in borders or patterns.
• Maiden-hair fern stems. These are a very good black, unfading and glossy. They are used for wrapping splints in twined basketry and for ornamentation.
• Grasses. All kinds of long grasses combine well with reeds, raffia, or other material. Excellent used in bundles, wrapped or sewn into coiled baskets.
• Pine Needles. Needles from the longleaf pine of the southern United States are desirable basket materials. Bundles of needles sewn with matching linen carpet thread are excellent for the coiled basket method. Equally fragrant and attractive used in the dried brown or cured green color.
• Straw and straw braids. Any variety of straw that is not too brittle when dried works well. Straw usually has a good yellow tone.
• Bamboo in many forms. Outside or inside peel, unsplit or split into matchstick size or strips of several widths, makes interesting weaving material.
• Birch bark. Peeled layers are used in strips.
• Cedar bark. Inside layers can be soaked and pounded and made almost as pliable as a yarn. Cut strips of different widths and thickness can also be used as splints or wefts.
• Wood slats. Many different kinds of wood can be made into narrow, thin slats for blinds and mats.

EMBELLISHMENTS — ORNAMENTATION

Bits and pieces or large areas are sometimes enhanced by the addition of other items, such as beads, feathers, leather, shells, mirror, metal, scraps of cloth. Apparently anything that stays in place, that provides a color or texture or adds to a design element desired by the craftsman, was and is applied. Sometimes other materials are introduced into the weave. Sewing on, appliqué, tying are methods used to add these various accents.

METHODS AND VOCABULARY OF BASKET WEAVING

Since we have discussed the role of basketry in general as a forerunner of textile weaving, in a book about weaving it seems suitable to also say something about the many techniques of weaving used in basketry.

Methods of forming a basket are almost as numerous as the variety of materials and shapes, and while basketry employs many of the same techniques used in cloth weaving, it has its own vocabulary. It may interest you to know some of the equivalent terms:

Cloth weaving	Basket weaving vocabulary
Warp	Stakes, or spokes
Weft	Weaver
Supplementary or added warps	Bi-stakes (added stakes for strength)
Warping the Loom	Setting up: fixing the stakes in place or preparing the button in coiling.
Plain weave	Randing (English term)
Double weft	Pairing, or slew
Pick, shot, or row of weaving	Stroke, or stitch
Twining technique	Twining, or chain-pairing

Methods

Weaving over and under on stiff stakes or spokes. *Weaving over and under* with braided or twisted material.

Winding — such as for handles. A strip of material is wound around a core, which can be bundles of grasses or reeds, or cord. Winding may be solid, or spaced so that the core shows.

Fitching. Open work, comparable to lace or leno weaves. Open spaces may be squares or rectangles, V'd or crosses.

Coiling. Bundles of short or soft pliable material (grasses, pine needles) wound with a strip material. (See Winding.) The thread or raffia used to sew with is usually an important design element. It is chosen carefully for color, either matching or a contrast, done neatly and with designed spacing. The Lazy Stitch alternates short and long stitches above and below the row for a distinctive pattern.

Figure-eight stitch. Over and under, crossing between rows.

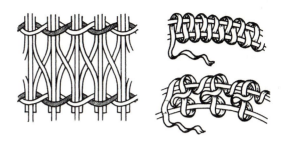

2-2. Fitching and twining. A row of twining is put in, then the stakes are crossed and left unwoven. A row of twining is woven below the open space. This is the same twining technique used for bags, but for bags the rows are pressed closely together.

2-3. Figure-eight stitch. Used in sewing and coiling baskets.

2-4. Knot, Lace, or Mariposa stitch. May be used when sewing coiled baskets, either with rows close together, or slightly apart to let the knot show. Drawing by Micheal Moshier.

Knot stitch. Lace or Mariposa stitch. A row of knots between rows of coils. Related to the Lazy Stitch. The knot occurs when the long stitch of the Lazy Stitch is crossed, thus a knot is below every other stitch. Very decorative, and can be used in open or closed work.

Twining. Simple twining is a pair of wefts moving together over the warp, twisting between warps, and enclosing each warp as shown in figure 2-2. Twining has been developed into a very sophisticated technique employing the use of intricate patterns and color changes. Indians of the Pacific Northwest made very fine baskets as well as coarse mats in twining. Taaniko weaving of the Maori is a twining variation; these people have made an art form of it in the interplay of colors and patterns, using multiple pairs of wefts and extra wefts carried along the back to be brought up when needed to complete a pattern.

Some of the methods are similar to others, but have different names and different applications. Some are named for the people who used them in their own particular way; some for the kind of weave, like the Herringbone finishing edge. This is woven with a narrow splint weaving back and forth in the last sewn row in a herringbone pattern.

AN OLD BASKETRY BOOK

In the hope that you might be able to find a copy in a library or somewhere, I'd like to tell you about a book that was given to me. It must have been published in the early 1920's. The book is *Practical Basket Making* by George Wharton James, Pasadena, California, who was also the publisher. It is a storehouse of information, filled with good photographs of model baskets and directions for weaving each one. Mr. James organized "The Basket Fraternity" as a means of communication and exchange of information between basket collectors and weavers. Basket weaving seems to have been taken more seriously as a craft in earlier days, with imaginative designing and careful work and study. I liked his "Eternal Waste Basket." He named it this because it was so strong it would last forever. I like to think it could mean because we always need one! If any of my readers know anything about Mr. James and his Basket Fraternity, I would be pleased to hear about it.

NEW DIRECTIONS

Much of the summer camp and therapy basket weaving follows the same old pattern of round reeds, baskets started on wooden bases, and no fresh design elements. They are fine, and fun, but when the whole range of basketry is surveyed, it is clear that there are many lovely forms and different ways to create them. I'd like to see some new approaches to basket work, such as textile weavers are bringing to their ancient craft. Most baskets are an honest expression of function and use of the material. By its nature, some basket material is limited in use because of stiffness, length of strand, or brittleness. How ingenious basket workers are in the way they use their raw materials is shown in our many photographs of baskets.

Baskets are habit-forming! Once you use and appreciate the endless possibilities in designs and materials, you are captive. They just naturally appeal to weavers. Only a part of the author's large collection is pictured — possession is rationalized because it is really a working collection! Not only are they decorative, but they serve to hold yarns, flowers, plants, and foods; they are used for shopping, as purses, for toting books, for picnics, and for weaving in progress. Old or new — lasting or expendable — baskets are very useful objects.

The baskets and mats shown in our photographs are from the Philippines, Taiwan, Italy, Mexico, Pakistan, Japan, Portugal, Ireland, Hawaii, England, India, Canada, and the United States. How true that baskets and raw materials are everywhere! Raffia, reeds of many indigenous varieties, bamboo in many forms, split and whole; willow, thin wooden splints; fibers from pineapple leaves, palm leaves, sea grasses; rushes from the Shannon River, Squaw grass, hemp, cedar bark — all these and more are used in basketry.

Baskets made by Pacific Northwest and Alaskan Indians (figure 2-5)

The patterned covered bottle from Alaska is very finely woven of shiny grasses, some of which have been dyed bright red and green. Some rows are open work. The cover is made separately, like a miniature basket, with a medallion-like design on the top. The covered basket, also from Alaska, almost as fine as the bottle, has inlaid wolf heads in different colors. The lid has a hole in the center and rows of differently colored borders.

2-5. Pacific Northwest and Alaskan Indian baskets.

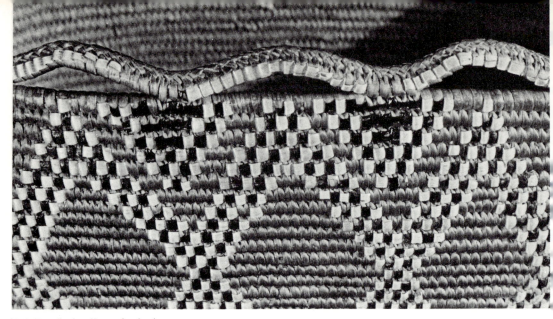

2-6. Detail of scallop-edge basket.

In the center is a hat made for the author by Mattie Howeattle, a Makah Indian, who was over one hundred years old at the time she wove it! It is made of finely split cedar bark, very flexible. The warm natural red-brown is embellished with an overlay pattern of two war canoes and two ducks of white grass. The edge is lacy open work. Patterned from the Coast Indian rain hats, it is reminiscent of a Chinese Coolie hat.

The open weave handled basket of hazel twigs is rigid and perfectly done; a good example of fitching, with the twigs held together by spaced rows of twining, with one row crossed for a decorative effect. The handle and top edge are wound.

The two oval baskets and the large rectangular one are so firm and evenly made that they are rigid and watertight. The patterns are put in by imbrication, so they show only on the outside. The large basket is cedar, with patterns in pale yellow and dark brown grass. For added strength and for decoration, the top has a row of solid braid, woven and sewn to form a shallow scallop. A detail is reproduced (figure 2-6) to show the beautifully even work of both the edge and the basket itself.

The two oval baskets are of lighter color spruce root, with all-over imbricated patterns of shiny pale straw color, black and brown. The top edges of these two are firmly finished with a row of tightly woven herringbone weave.

All the baskets depicted in figure 2-5 are from the collection of Gladys McIlveen. (Photograph by Kent Kammerer.)

Italy and Taiwan

A perfect example of good craftsmanship and a knowing combination of materials is the leather-topped basket from Italy, pictured in figure 2-7. Made with strong rattan handles and stakes, a weft of tough outside peel, and covered with a beautifully made hinged and lined saddle leather top. The button holding the leather loop is made of a chestnut. This, too, serves to hold yarns. The delicate scrolled ring is the inside headpiece to hold the large flat-topped sun and rain hats worn by Taiwan women. The tray is raffia. The other baskets are made of flat splints, round reeds, sea grass, and raffia. Sewn coils, lacy open work, and raffia in an intricate sewn pattern. Collection of the author. (Photograph by Kent Kammerer.)

From the Philippines, Mexico, and Portugal (figure 2-8)

Wide palm leaves, plain weave, make a square covered basket from the Philippines. The long, narrow basket from Mexico is in coil technique using the lace knotted stitch. The shallow, coiled and sewn plate has rows placed to make a pleasant pinwheel design. The small square reed basket has a hinged cover, held by a figure-eight fastener, secured with a double loop of bamboo. The graceful oval basket of flat, shiny material is made in Portugal, but seems to be the all-time favorite shopping basket in Ireland! As so many baskets

2-7. Italian and Taiwan baskets.

2-8. Philippine, Mexican, and Portuguese baskets.

2-9. Taiwan, Philippine, and domestic baskets.

40

2-10. Basketry from far and wide.

are, this style is made in a whole nest of sizes — even one that can be used as a portable and comfortable carrier for a tiny baby. The open-weave basket stitch is like that used in cane seating — crossed and interlaced. Collection of the author. (Photograph by Kent Kammerer.)

Two from Taiwan

The layered Bride's Basket is made in many sizes, some of them very large, to hold a whole wardrobe of folded garments. This one holds yarns, weaving shuttles, and bobbins. Firm and finely woven of split reed, dyed a light, warm brown. The wide splint handle is held in shape with woven areas, and the sturdy hand-hold is also woven on in a decorative way. The little braided animals are hemp. (Figure 2-9.)

Three from the Philippines

The graceful, petal-like basket is woven with a combination of open work and winding in dull and shiny reed and bamboo with decorative bands reinforcing the bottom and center. A strainer-

basket has a wooden branch, peeled and whittled to form the handle and rim. Done with braided edge and fine bamboo woven over splints. Small carrying basket with twisted and braided handles, made of soft raffia-like leaves in natural gray-green to straw colors. (Figure 2-9.)

Domestic

The familiar bleached reeds of our camp and therapy baskets, center. This one was woven on a wooden base. Collection of the author. (Photograph by Kent Kammerer.) (Figure 2-9.)

A mixed group of basketry (figures 2-10 — 13)

Each one is suitably designed for its use and material. From Japan comes a picturesque and comfortable garden hat made of bundles of fine grass sewn round and round, with a firm braided and reinforced edge. As you work in your garden, you can peer through the few inches of open work weaving at the front edge. The small, covered trinket basket was woven by a Makah Indian on the Olympic Peninsula. Also from Japan: the stiff-han-

41

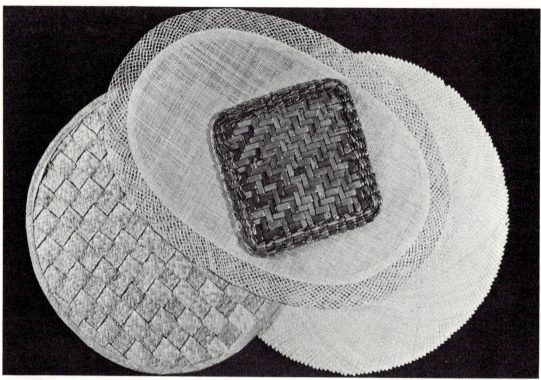

2-11. Mats made of basket materials.
2-12. Japanese grass mat.

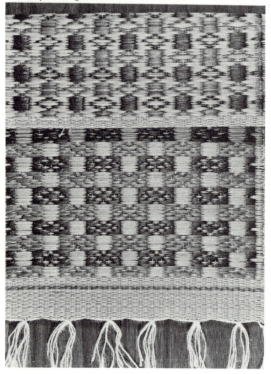

dled basket of fine split bamboo is a tea strainer; hair ornament and fly-swatter made of bamboo; the firm tray, swan, napkin ring, and small rice basket, all woven from round reeds and split bamboo. The tiny bottle is covered with raffia and contains English lavender. Collection of the author. (Photograph by Kent Kammerer.) (Figure 2-10.)

Mats made from fibers used in baskets are shown in figure 2-11. The fine lauhala mat from Hawaii was woven from narrow strips of palm leaves; the technique of weaving in the round forms an attractive edge of small points. The oval mat, plain weave with applied lacy weave edge is piña cloth from the Philippines, described in Chapter 1. The square hot-dish pad was woven in Ireland from rushes that grow along the Shannon River; the twill-weave center is of flat strips, the border is plain weave of narrow folded strips. Although they varnish these, the natural variations of the brown and green tones of the reeds come through. The round mat in plain weave was woven of braided strips about an inch wide, made from thin narrow strips of material. A binding is stitched around the edge. Collection of the author. (Photograph by Kent Kammerer.)

2-13. Basket-weave seat woven on a stool.

A fine, flexible grass mat from Keuashiki, Japan (figure 2-12) is a softer, more refined version of the plain and twill weave tatami mats the Japanese use as floor coverings. Mercerized cotton warp, loom-controlled pattern. The weft is soft, pliable grass in narrow strips. Some is natural gray-green shaded into brown. The pattern weft is the same grass dyed black and red. Note that at the top of the picture a portion of the mat is turned down to show the difference in pattern on the reverse side.

The selvedge is neat and decorative, with the ends of weft woven back in and closely clipped. Groups of eight warps are tied in a simple knot to finish off the ends. Courtesy Zada Sigman. (Photograph by Kent Kammerer.)

Figure 2-13 shows a seat woven directly on the wooden frame of a folding stool. Done in four-over-four basket weave, warp and weft of twisted fiber. Collection of the author. (Photograph by Kent Kammerer.)

RELATING BASKET WEAVING TO TEXTILES

Figure 2-14 shows a weaving exercise to develop a textile for a pillow, using different weaves: two-over-two and three-over-three basket weave combined with single plain weave. The result is an interesting variation of a check. Student work, Seattle Pacific College. Teacher, Larry Metcalf, Assistant Professor, Art Department, Seattle Pacific College, Seattle. (Photograph by Larry Metcalf.)

Basket weaves and designs from carefully woven Indian baskets are inspiration for textile weavers. Gladys McIlveen, retired social worker with the United States Bureau of Indian Affairs, has worked with the Pacific Northwest Indians for years. She translates patterns from lovely old baskets into small tapestries. She wove the four shown in figures 2-15, 16 on small finished picture frames, five by seven inches, and left them right on the frame looms. Swedish Tapestry Knot technique. Courtesy, Gladys McIlveen. (Photograph by Kent Kammerer.)

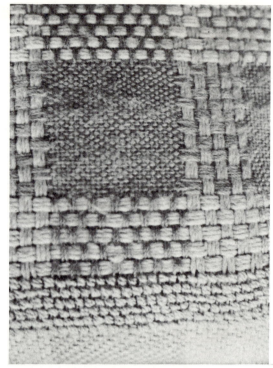

2-14. Plain and basket weave combined.

2-15. Tapestry designs from Indian baskets.

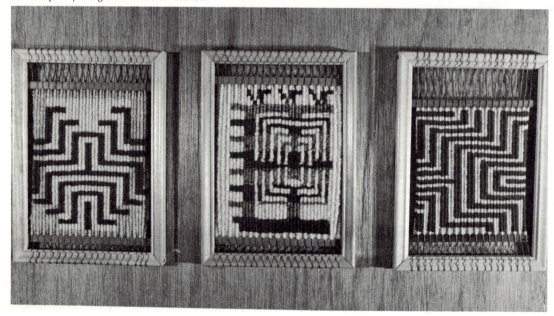

44

2-16. Tapestry designs from Indian baskets.

2-17. Woven mats — cattail, plantain, wormwood.

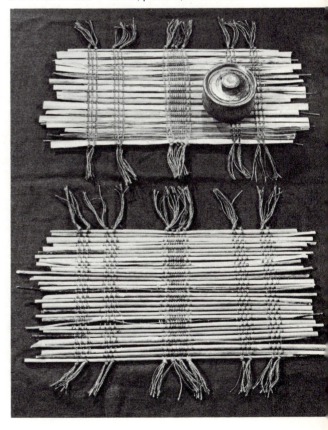

WEAVING WITH NATURAL WEFTS

Patricia Wilson, Seattle, enjoys designing and weaving with natural materials and is doing a detailed study of them. When she cruises in the Pacific Northwest waters, she goes ashore and searches out interesting wefts. Here are just a few of the handsome things she does with them.
Figure 2-17, top. Cattail leaves and plantain.
Bottom. Cattail stalks and wormwood.

Cattail leaves and stalks were utilized to a great extent by the Coast Indians in this region. Notice how well these mats blend in with the look — and the weight — of hand-made pottery.

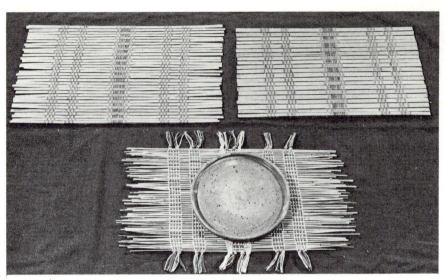

2-18. Birch slats. Cedar slats. Grasses.

2-19. Fine linen combined with natural wefts.

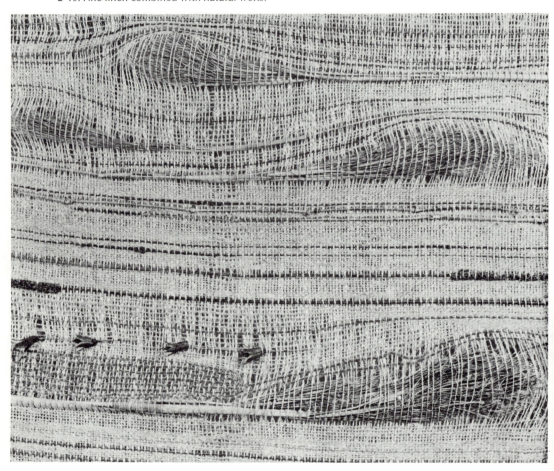

Figure 2-18, top left. Birch slats stained in a drift-wood finish.

Top right. Cedar slats weathered naturally.

Bottom. Rye, orchard, and canary grasses.

All of these mats are woven with a minimum of warp, in well-spaced bands. The natural materials are the feature.

Figure 2-19. Combined with fine linen warp and weft, panic grass, dwarf bamboo, rhododendron seedpods, and plantain are woven into a very fine decorative panel.

A good example of how the weft can be mod-eled around a shape and follow curving contours. The weft, here, follows the curve of the brushy end of the plantain stalk, capturing it in a cage made by the warp.

Mrs. Wilson has written several articles, published in the *Handweaver and Craftsman Magazine* recently, detailing her experiences in finding and preparing her weft materials, and how she weaves them. Courtesy, Patricia Wilson. (Photographs by William Eng, Audio Visual Services, University of Washington.)

2-20. Drawing of a coiled mat, by Micheal Moshier.

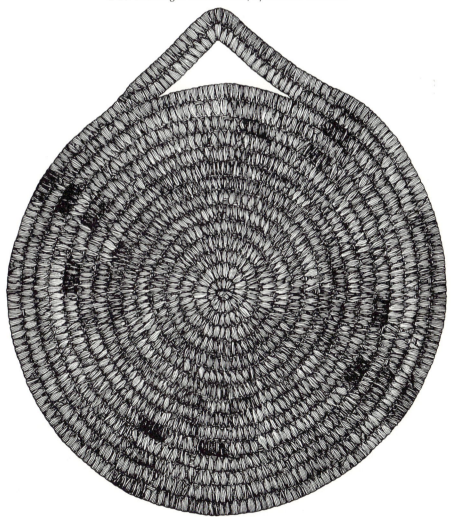

Handwoven Cloth
of Many Kinds

A wide variety of handwoven fabrics are pictured and explained in this chapter to give you some idea of the many ways textiles can be enriched by introducing a loom-woven pattern, by colors, or by the use of interesting yarns. Except where noted, these were all woven on floor looms with at least four heddles, a reed and beater, and foot treadles. Patterns were threaded into the heddles, controlled by the treadles and reed, to form the design. Many of them could be woven on a small loom — note that some were — as a matter of interest, a challenge, to develop a textile design, or just to discover how the weaving was done. Perhaps they will give you a starting point for designing a fabric. Perhaps all textiles will become more interesting as you become familiar with them and learn to recognize weaves, patterns, and yarns discussed in other chapters.

The romance of handweaving and the development of the textile industry is a fascinating subject, reaching far back in history. In America, handweaving began through necessity when the Pilgrims landed from the Mayflower, and pioneer homes soon became miniature textile factories.

All members of the family were needed — even the little ones helped with the carding and preparation of the wool, cotton, and flax. Development of tools and machines to prepare fibers, to spin, and to weave progressed — sometimes slowly — but steadily. In time, as machines began to produce textiles in large quantities, the homely tasks of hand spinning and weaving gradually declined and looms and spinning wheels were stored in attics.

In our day, we undertake these activities by choice, not from need, and therefore making beautiful things from yarn becomes a pleasant, satisfying occupation and creative outlet.

PLAIN WEAVE DOES NOT HAVE TO LOOK PLAIN!

• A subtle and irregular check is created by the several colors and weights of yarn in the warp, crossed by smooth and nubby weft yarns (figure 3-1). The heavy cotton nub is the same as that in the warp. But it *is* just a plain weave.

3-1. Plain weave in smooth and nubby yarn.

3-2. Plain weave in cotton, rayon, and wool.

- Plain weave but not plain (figure 3-2). Dull, nubby spun cotton and lustrous rayon novelty spin combined with two smooth spun cottons and one wool, in closely related warm beige, grayed orange, and gold tones.
- Yellow and brown cotton (figure 3-3). Check arrangement of two colors in the warp, the same two colors in the weft. Interest is in the changing proportion of widths by use of different numbers of warps and wefts. This creates a variation on a plain, measured check. Weaver, Marilyn King. Teacher, Mrs. Dorothy Stickney, Renton High School, Washington. (Photograph by William Eng.)
- Another check. Here unequal division lines form rectangles and squares (figure 4). Different shades are used for further variation. Weaver, Solange Kowert. (Photograph, Audio Visual Services, University of Washington.)

3-3. Plain weave check.

3-4. Plain weave rectangles and squares.

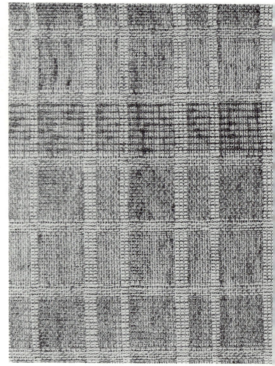

3-5. Plain, basket, and twill weaves combined.

3-6. Stripes in plain, basket, and twill weaves.

COMBINATION OF WEAVES

• Plain, basket, and twill weaves: the irregular size of the unspun wool gives an unstudied texture (figure 3-5). Bedspread or upholstery weight.
• Plain, basket, and twill weaves make a stripe (figure 3-6). Plain weave is in smooth wool, the other weaves in smooth and nub yarn.

3-7. Strong color contrast in plain and twill weaves.

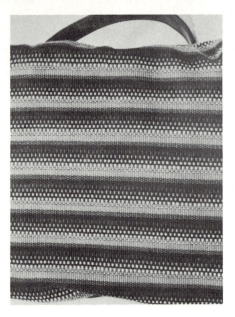

3-8. Heavy ribbed weave, linen and jute.

• With strongly contrasting colors — navy blue and white weft on a light turquoise blue warp — a changing striped pattern is achieved by plain weave and twill weave (figure 3-7). The border pattern occurs by alternating the dark and light rows, always putting the same color in the same shed. Yarns here are very fine, slightly nubbed rayon/cotton on a mercerized warp. Figures 3-5, 6, 7 woven by the author. (Photograph by Kent Kammerer.)

• Warp stripes in a heavy ribbed weave for a tote bag (figure 3-8). Linen and jute. Change of color is one way to create a dimensional effect. The fabric looks deeply ridged. Weaver, Jeannette Lund. (Photograph, Audio Visual Services, University of Washington.)

3-9. Four-shaft twill.

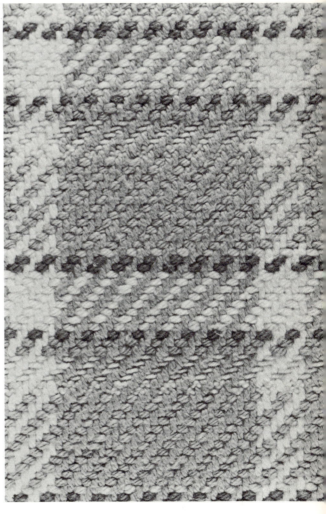

3-10. Twill plaid in heavy cotton yarn.

TWILLS AND VARIATIONS OF TWILLS

• Ordinary four-shaft twill (figure 3-9). Weft stripes in light yellow, brown, and yellow-orange on a fine cream wool warp. Note the different slant in each of the three areas. At top, the weft is the size of worsted knitting yarn. Below, the dark stripe is quite fine wool. This is an interesting sampling exercise with any pattern. Weave a few inches each in several sizes of yarn to see the variations in spacing and angles. (Photograph by Kent Kammerer.)

• Twill. A plaid formed by warp stripes, using different colors in the same heavy cotton yarn. Weft is in different colors and several sizes of cotton yarn. (Photograph by Kent Kammerer.) (3-10.)

• Twill variation. Herringbone. Two colors. Warp and weft are both the same cotton ratine (figure 3-11). Weaver, Ruth Clarke. (Photograph by Kent Kammerer.)

• Twill variation. Broken Twill. Wool and mohair coat fabric (figure 3-12). Weaver, Sylvia Tacker. (Photograph by Harold Tacker.)

3-12. Broken twill: wool and mohair.

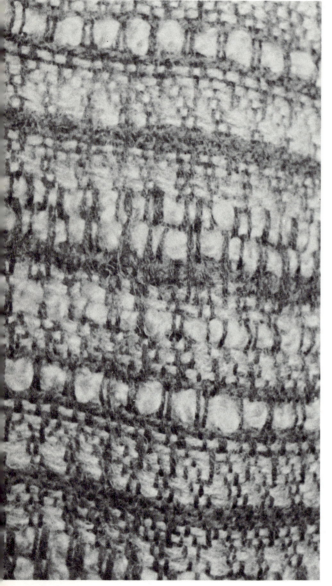

3-11. Herringbone in cotton ratine.

3-13. Monk's Belt threading, fine to worsted wool yarns.

3-14. Warp skips used for Roman blind.

WOVEN PATTERNS, LOOM-CONTROLLED

• Monk's Belt threading. Weft is white wool and all color and pattern is in the warp (figure 3-13). Warp yarns are greens, red-orange, yellow, white, and dark brown. Several sizes of yarn from very fine wool to worsted size and some novelty nub spins are used. Woven by the author. (Photograph by Kent Kammerer.)

• Warp skips create an interesting pattern of straight woven bands alternating with unwoven weft, which dips slightly, to give an undulating airy look, with some light coming through (figure 3-14). A Roman blind — it folds up like an accordian. Weaver, Jan Burhen. (Photograph, Audio Visual Services, University of Washington.)

55

3-15. Float weave.

3-16. Honeycomb suit fabric.

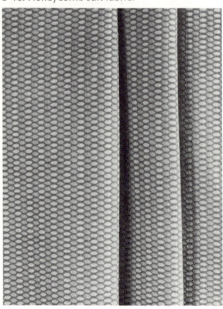

• Float or Overshot weave. Two colors, two sizes of cotton yarn. The pattern overlays the background, with a good play of shadow (figure 3-15). Woven by the author. (Photograph by Kent Kammerer.)

• Honeycomb. An old favorite pattern, and one which can be used in dozens of variations in size of design units and yarns. Figure 3-16 shows a suit fabric in rich red tones, very fine wool. Each little honeycomb unit is small, so the over-all look is of texture. Two related values of red in alternate warp stripes. This was an award winner in a Northwest Craftsman annual exhibit at the Henry Gallery, University of Washington. Weaver, Alice Streutker. (Photograph, Audio Visual Services, University of Washington.)

• Honeycomb upholstery fabric of heavy wool and fine cotton (figure 3-17). Large and small units of the pattern alternate. Weaver, Sara Gossard. (Photograph by Kent Kammerer.)

• Double weave. Deep, rich texture done in warm red and orange tones (figure 3-18). Wool. Weaver, Laurie Herrick. (Photograph, Audio Visual Services, University of Washington.)

• Bird's eye (twill). White wool on light orange mercerized cotton warp (figure 3-19). Woven by the author. (Photograph by Kent Kammerer.)

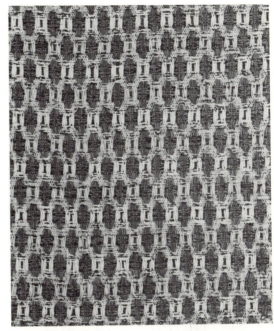

3-18. Double weave.

3-19. Bird's eye twill.

3-17. Honeycomb upholstery fabric.

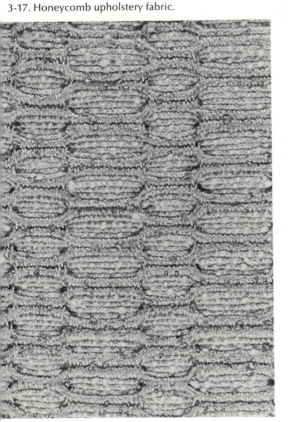

3-20. Novelty spins for surface interest.

• A group of fabrics woven with different yarns (figure 3-20). Pattern or surface interest is achieved simply by the use of slub and novelty spins and colors added to warp or weft. All are plain weave except the two at the bottom, which are twill and broken twill. Woven by the author. (Photograph by Kent Kammerer.)

• Clara Chapman uses her loom as a prime part of her designing of textiles. She commands many harnesses, knows just what the loom can and should do, and goes on from there to weave lovely rich fabrics, which are always right for the purpose. The four photographs shown in figures 3-21, 22, 23, 24 are all from her fabrics, and we regret that we could not show them in color because the subtle color-play is so much a part of their handsomeness. (Photographs by Kent Kammerer.)

An original Greek key design worked out by Clara Chapman (figure 3-21). Summer and winter threading, on twelve harnesses. Pattern weft is gold rayon boucle. Background is a deep, vibrant blue composed of alternating strong royal blue and very dark green-blue cotton and linen. Weft is a dark grayed blue. Background is tabby, or plain weave. Pattern is woven in stripes of increasing width.

3-21. Twelve-harness Greek key design. Clara Chapman.

3-22. Coat fabrics. Clara Chapman.

3-23. Six-harness twill variations. Clara Chapman.

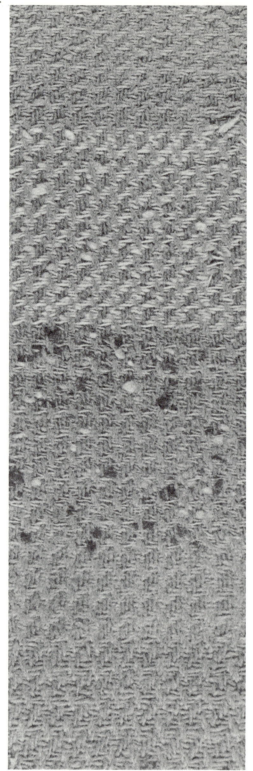

Three wools — all for coats (figure 3-22). Top, plain weave, silk and wool; heavy wool yarn every few rows makes a ridge. Center, twill of handspun wool, a hairy mohair, and fine wool spun together; the two mohair colors in warp and weft almost weave a hound's tooth check against a smooth yarn background. Bottom, white looped mohair and wool yarn make a crepey, soft, light coating in twill weave.

A sampling strip of six-harness twill variations, figure 3-23. Different treadlings and use of color produce subtle diversities. Two shades of muted orange with gray-green; one section in tweed nub yarn, which changes the look of the weave. Notice the section where small areas of the darker color are framed in diagonal bands.

3-24. Eight-harness twill variations. Clara Chapman.

Very much a part of our American hand-craft heritage are the handwoven coverlets of early Colonial days. Each style of weaving has a reason for being, and a charm all its own, an expression of rightness for the time, the people, the situation. Crisp, light mattings are right for hot climates where grassy materials are abundant. The heavy pile Scandinavian rug fabrics brought warmth and color to long, cold winters of that land. Just so, Colonial coverlets were right for their time and place. They were handsome by day, on the bed in the main room of the home, and warm by night.

The romance of American coverlet weaving, at its height when the Colonies were being settled, should not be forgotten. It is a part of all weaving, and the total American craft scene, no matter if you weave nothing but three-dimensional constructions from synthetic yarns! The Colonials spun wool from their own sheep, raised cotton, and flax for linen, made their own dyes of natural materials such as hickory and butternuts for brown, blue from indigo.

3-25. Eighteenth century Pennsylvania coverlet, cotton and wool, double weave. Pattern of interlocking circles. (Courtesy of the Philadelphia Museum of Art.)

Eight-harness twill, figure 3-24. Warm camel tan with dots of orange slub wool. The yarns lie on slightly different levels which gives depth and shadow, providing little frames for the orange dot that appears in every small square. The hand of this suiting is light and soft, and it is very wearable.

61

Even though the all-over designs used in coverlets were rigidly limited by the right-angle crossing of warp and weft, patterns were devised with an illusion of curves and circles. Stepped outlines, interlocking lines woven in fine yarns create patterns with circles, ovals and wavering lines. Many of the warp patterns came from Europe, but some were unknown there and are as American as our apple pie and hamburgers! Clothing and household textiles were needed, so they were woven by hand from materials grown and prepared by the householder. In simple homes, although it was in daily use, the patterned coverlet or counterpane was often the only decorative, beautiful thing the family owned.

Weaving directions — draughts (we now call them drafts) — were designed or borrowed, and then passed along as treasures to family and friends. They were enclosed in letters, sent by riders braving all kinds of hardships. They were marked down on small scraps of precious paper and kept in the family Bible or with important documents. Some were detailed on odd scraps of paper, sewn together. Often the drafts were hoarded and kept secret, so one family alone could enjoy a prized pattern. Happenings, history, wishful dreams — even the weather — all are reflected in the names given to these woven counterpanes and coverlets, which were such cherished household possessions.

NAMES AND WEAVES

The names of very old weaving patterns, especially those used in the Colonial coverlets are sometimes descriptive, sometimes a puzzle — a kind of "inside family joke." It's fun to read about them and quote them, to look at pictures and try to solve the mystery of the name, to imagine why that distant weaver chose *that* name for her pattern. Some are easy: "Wheel," "Bird's-eye," "Waffle" — but why "Missouri Trouble"? A commonly used weave named "Summer and Winter" was an all-American idea with tabby foundation and pattern thread closely interwoven. This is a double-face weave, like two layers, one overlaying the other, connected with interlacement of threads along the edges of the design units. Since the coverlet was reversible, the name probably came from the practice of putting the dark-patterned side up for the cold months, the light pattern up in the sum-

mer. They were usually dark blue and white. In old weaving books, most likely to be found in libraries or museums, you will find drafts, sketches, and pictures of the old coverlets along with stories and names. *The Shuttle-craft Book of American Hand-Weaving* by the late Mary Meigs Atwater is one. Originally published in 1928, reprinted in 1943, revised edition published by Macmillan in 1951, it has a wealth of information about these strictly American weavings, drafts for reconstructing them on your own loom, and tales about the long history of weaving.

Some of the coverlet names

The nature of the names with which the early settlers endowed their creations reveals a people of wit and imagination despite the rigors of their life. Topical names reflecting the current news were popular: Tennessee Trouble, Lee's Surrender, Perry's Victory, Bonaparte's March, Indian War. Names from the natural surroundings were also much favored: Sunflower — which looks like a large seed center, formed by tiny dots in the weave; Sunrise, an old American pattern with rays spreading out from the center; Dog Tracks — dark alternating with light squares, it does look a little like a pad print; Goose Eye, Raindrops, Bird's Nest, Pine Tree. Snail Trail has meandering lines, disciplined, but wandering. Twenty-five Snowballs speaks for itself. Star of Bethlehem shows a four-pointed star, much like those pictured on Christmas cards. Whig Rose — a very ancient pattern. And, simply — World's Wonder!

Others were apparently either inspired by or named after something familiar which they suggested: Orange Peel — rows of parenthesis-shaped lines; Church Windows — like small rose windows and squares; Bow knot; Box-in-a-bush; Cup and Saucer — circles within a square; Doors and Windows.

We also found Philadelphia Pavement, Wheel of Fortune, Chariot Wheel, and combinations like Snowball and Pine Tree, Wheel and Star, Lover's Knot with Window Sash! And then — there is Job's Perplexity and The Bachelor.

3-26. A modern Op-art weaving from an old coverlet design. Hope Munn worked out the threading and wove this panel in black and white. (Photograph by Kent Kammerer.)

Learning by Doing

A NOTE TO TEACHERS OF WEAVING

Here are gleanings from talks with and answers to questions asked of teachers in grades fourth to twelfth and through college level, and university students and teachers in summer school learning how to weave. Several teachers used a draft of this chapter in their weaving programs, making helpful comments. Young weavers were also observed and helped while at work.

• Most teachers seemed to think that paper weaving is a very good way to start. Some think youngsters can cope with paper a little more easily than with yarn, at first.

• Young children handle the paper strips well. They enjoy it. The weaving goes fast.

• It is a good beginning for color relationships and proportion.

• They want more ideas. (We show a number of photographs here, and you will find a helpful chapter full of ideas in *Crafts Design* by Moseley, Johnson and Koenig, Wadsworth Publishing Co., Belmont, Calif., 1962.)

• Weaving projects often bog down when beginners plunge into it without really knowing the basic steps and what it is all about.

• The sampling idea is good. It's appeal and scope and attention value will vary with ages and interests. Some children might like to do just an inch or two of each weave in a long strip. Others might want to do separate squares to be put into a notebook, mounted separately, or combined into a wall hanging. One teacher said her fourth graders were excited about and completed with enthusiasm a combined group wall-hanging, with each student effort proudly included. Learning the importance of sampling will be of help later when a "real" project is woven. Present the sampling as a necessary step before real weaving can begin.

• Show your students examples of good weaving of all kinds. Some will be inspired to try something far beyond their beginner's ability, but will happily do some sampling to learn how to go on. One ten-year-old boy wanted to do a copy of the "People tapestry" on the jacket of *Weaving is for Anyone.* He tried, found he must learn to weave first, and went back to something easier for a start.

• Sampling can be kept to a minimum or expanded as time and interest permits. Then, at a certain time, it is important to make some Thing — preferably a pictorial weaving — something to take home, to use, to show. (See "Student Experiences," page 92.) A class banner would be fun, each one weaving a section. This will include planning a design, color, weaving, sewing, decorative stitchery — and teamwork. Colors and yarns can be planned for harmony, a general idea or theme worked out, and then each weaver will go on his own. Some will want to weave plain areas, some will be ambitious to try patterns and textures and pictorial weavings.

• Perhaps the students will want to weave individual small projects. A little collar for a pet dog or cat; a tiny blanket for a tiny doll; a large doll

. Faces. Tapestry woven by the author. (Photograph by Phil Davidson.)

blanket from several small units, joined; doll pillows, pincushions, coasters, hotpads, purses, place mats. A little wool pocket — perhaps with an initial or decoration woven in — for mother or teacher to help sew onto a sweater or skirt. A small picture-weaving put into a deep frame or hung from stick or dowel is a grand present for best friend or family. Pillows, puppy blankets, headbands, bookmarkers, and guitar straps are all pleasing projects.

You will find a wide span of interest in this craft, ranging from those who reluctantly do a minimum piece to those who race through the samples, get on with a pictorial weaving, and then do several different weavings at home on their own.

Class experiences

Several quite different class experiences in weaving are detailed in the following pages. Bothersome points are taken up in "General Hints," and, hopefully, are adequately covered, since techniques become familiar and tend to be taken for granted by the experienced.

For this long-time weaver, the opportunity to observe and help student weavers was a revelation — and reward. Have fun teaching.

— Jean Wilson.

THE WEAVING ACTION

A loom is the frame that holds the warp threads in tension, so wefts can be woven to form cloth. There are as many variations of looms as there are countries and cultures. In this book, however, we are more concerned with learning about yarns and textiles than about various kinds of looms. (See "Preface," on looms.)

You can create cloth in a limited way on just a frame or a piece of cardboard. Such equipment is readily available, inexpensive, and has proved to be adequate for use in a classroom and for sampling. However, weaving on cardboard looms or simple frames is not an end in itself — it is a means to an end. These small looms are merely tools for learning techniques.

The basic process of weaving is the same, whether on a scrap of cardboard or on a ninety-inch loom for weaving bedspreads. The warp must be held taut. The weft must go over and under the warp threads and be beaten in. Weaving a wide piece of cloth by putting the weft over the warps

one by one takes a long time and becomes q boring. That is why looms have ways to raise lower all of the warp yarns.

For production and wide widths, the loom n become more of a machine and have hel added, such as heddles to help open the shed form the patterns; foot treadles to move the h dles up and down; a beater the width of the lc to beat the yarns in evenly; beams to hold the warp and the finished cloth. When you we over and under warps with a needle or bobbi weft, you are acting as the heddle, making a shed by lifting one or a few warps at a time. Y fingers, fork, or comb act as the beater.

GENERAL HINTS

From experience, from questions asked, and f watching weavers at work, we have found the lowing to be puzzling to beginning weavers.

Planning

Weavers must look ahead and plan carefully fore even selecting a loom and yarns to we with. After you know what you are going weave, you choose the loom that is suitable the right kind of yarns for the piece. You must the spacing of the warp, the weaving met (plain, pattern, tapestry, etc.) and decide how want the ends finished. These things will dic the kind of loom you use and the way you and end your weaving. Your planning does have to be *absolutely* rigid; part of the fur weaving is changing and improvising, even in middle of it, and perhaps weaving something is better than your original plan. However, necessary to keep within the best limits of y loom, your yarn, and the planned use of what are making.

Before starting to weave

Decide how you will finish the ends. Will have a hem? Will the warp ends be cut and k ted into a fringe? Do you want the warp e lifted off and left uncut in loops? (See figure 4- Will a wall-hanging or tapestry be hung fro stick or dowel, in a hem or in woven tabs? W be lined? Each finish requires a different amc of warp left at the end. These decisions mak difference in the size of the loom and lengt the warp you will need. The technique and size of yarn determine how much extra warp you must allow for "take-up" in the weaving, or for weaving the piece a little larger than you want for the finished size. Most weaving relaxes some when it is released from the warp tension, and tends to become a bit smaller. Of course for place mats and items that will require a lot of laundering, you must be sure to weave your pieces large enough to allow for a little shrinkage.

Starting the weaving

Start your weaving on any kind of loom, using strips of cardboard, "throw-away" heavy yarn, and a few rows of plain weave. There are several very good reasons for this. It helps to space and stabilize the warp. On a small loom, it helps to even the tension. It gives a firm, straight row to weave against so your weaving will be square with the warp. It is a protector for the main weaving to keep it from raveling out after it is removed from the loom and has not been finished off. This throw-away yarn and weaving fills the warp and saves long ends for fringe or knotting. It gives added length to turn back into a hem.

What to do with the weft ends

The end of the weft is tucked in at the beginning of weaving by bringing it around the outside warp, weaving in over a few warps. The end can be trimmed off neatly after the weaving is finished. It will pack in and not be noticed. To make the cut end a little less bulky when using a large-sized yarn, cut the end at a slant. If you are using the very large rug roving, you can leave the cut end at the selvedge, not turned back. When the weaving is finished, the end can be cut off even with the edge. Sometimes this looks better than trying to turn it back in.

When you run out of yarn within a row and have to start another weft, always try to join it near the edge. Sometimes a joining can be almost hidden at the edge of a pattern in the weaving. In basket weave, or when you have two weft yarns in one shed, cut each of the ends a different length, slanting the cuts if necessary; then they won't both be at the same spot, making a lump.

Making a "waistline" — drawing in the sides

Try to keep your weaving even and the same width all of the way. This is especially important if you are doing a wall-hanging or tapestry, or anything where the edge shows. It is hard to do, and when you are a new weaver you will need to think about it all the time (in fact *all* weavers have to!). Keep the weft relaxed enough so it won't pull in the outside warp as you bring it around into the next row and beat it in. When you put it in the weft, slant it at an angle, make scallops in it, then ease it down into the row. (See figure 4-30.) This is called "bubbling." It takes practice to get the weft in there loose enough to keep it from pulling in but flat enough to keep it from popping up in little loops. It is worth spending some practice time on this. As you weave, check the line of the outside warps constantly, and keep them straight from top to bottom, as they were when you began the weaving. The line will come in some, but try not to get an edge that wanders in and out — unless that is a part of your design!

Doing the weaving

For a small loom it is usually easier to thread your weft yarns into a blunt tapestry needle. With short lengths of yarn, stick shuttles, small wound bobbins, or just fingers will all work depending upon what weaving you are doing.

When you weave a row of Ghiordes Knot loops, be sure that the first one at the edge where you tie it in, lies in the same direction as the rest of the row. And there always must be at least one row of plain weave between rows of knots and loops to help hold them in place.

If you want fine detail in a pictorial weaving, you must plan to use a fine warp, closely set, and fairly fine yarns in the weft. Large yarns are excellent for bold, abstract patterns, stripes, loops, and such, but they are too coarse to permit small details.

Weave comfortably! It may be easy for you to weave a row of continuous knots from left to right, but awkward coming back the other way. So do them the way that is best for you.

Weaving is usually started at the bottom of the loom and proceeds upwards. An exception is weaving or twining on a bag loom, which has a warp left loose at the bottom. Weavings on these are made from the top down. Watching young weavers at work on small looms, though, we have seen weaving done from the side, the top, the bottom, upside down, and backwards! Your design just might benefit from this freedom with a small loom that lets you weave in all directions.

Young weavers and many beginning weavers we noted weave the pattern or main design in a pictorial weaving first, filling in the background afterward. The question has been asked by teachers whether this is a good idea or even permissible. The answer is that if a weaver is learning the techniques of weaving in order to become a good craftsman and do a good job of it, it seems to me the proper procedures should be followed, but, when this has been done, the exact, precise procedures can be relaxed, just so the result is good and craftsmanship is well done.

Specifically, when weaving a tapestry, to do it in the proper way; the background and pattern are woven simultaneously so the color joinings and returns can be made at the right time in the right way. Weaving on a slant or curve, or any design unit that can be done in an isolated way, is possible. On sample-size wall hangings of heavy yarn it is quite easy to weave a central motif and then join the background neatly. As with most things, though, this all depends upon the exact piece being woven, and how important learning the techniques correctly seems to the teacher and to the student.

Before removing the weaving from the loom

If you are using warp loops for top and bottom selvedge on a small cardboard loom, be sure that you have enough rows crowded in at top and bottom to fill out the warp to the very edge.

If you plan to cut the warp, secure your weaving before cutting. Run a line of glue (Elmer's, No-Sew, etc.) along the last row of weaving and warp ends. Let dry thoroughly before cutting warps. Or, if you plan to knot the warp ends, start at one edge, cut just the number of threads you need, knot them, then cut the next group to be knotted.

If a hem has been woven and is to be turned back and sewn, glue or small knots will secure the ends; then a row of machine stitching can be run just above, the extra ends trimmed off and the raw edge turned in and hemmed.

If, for some reason, the weaving has been removed from the loom by cutting the warp, but you want to knot the warps, be sure you take each warp in order as it was on the loom, and be sure to include every warp. A few warp ends may have moved up into the woven part.

The main thing to keep in mind is: You don't want to risk losing any of the weaving at either end by having it ravel out after the warp has been cut from the loom, so some planning and precautions must be taken, as above.

WEAVING SAMPLES

If our hands work out a problem, we understand and remember it better, so let's do some sample weaving and learn how the different weaves really happen. This way you will find you can soon recognize different weaving patterns and you will have a better knowledge of how cloth is made.

Two suggestions for looms and sample weaving

a) Do each different weave on a small frame or cardboard loom (figure 4-1). Make each one a separate square, all the same size. These can then be mounted on a card or in a notebook, with the name of the weave, the yarn used, the number of warps per inch, and so on, for future reference. They can be planned to combine into a composition or hanging. All of our samples were woven this way, on a cardboard loom. We warped it all the way around and wove two samples with one warping. (See directions on page 70.)
or
b) Use a frame, 12 or 15 inches long, and weave only a few inches of each weave on this longer warp. Separate each example with a few rows of thread or a strip of cardboard, or leave open warp between, and be sure to secure the warp ends with a line of glue before cutting. Each weave can be tagged along the side for reference. Picture frames are satisfactory if the corners are reinforced, but canvas stretcher frames are best because they are very sturdy, are easily put together and come apart readily, and can be used over and over again in pairs of different sizes. These are available at art supply stores.

The 19-inch chipboard loom with pins (see page 98) worked out very well with rows of the different sampling weaves.

About weaving those samples

Generally speaking, it best to weave samples of a technique in fairly coarse yarn, not set too closely, so the beginning weaver can really see where the yarn goes and just what is happening. In our ex-

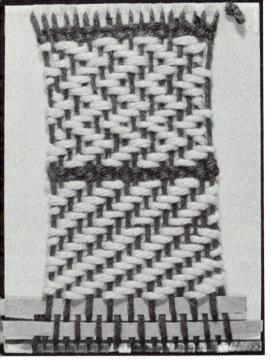

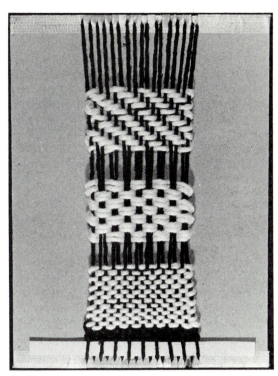

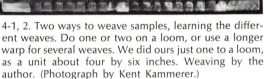

4-1, 2. Two ways to weave samples, learning the different weaves. Do one or two on a loom, or use a longer warp for several weaves. We did ours just one to a loom, as a unit about four by six inches. Weaving by the author. (Photograph by Kent Kammerer.)

amples, we used medium-size cotton/rayon rug yarn in just two contrasting colors, a light and a dark. This is the yarn available at most variety stores. We suggest it for this series of student samples. After doing the basic weaves and a few variations, the weavers can turn to wools and other yarns with exciting variety in textures, spins, and colors.

The simplest version of a weave is done by using exactly the same color and yarn for both warp and weft; you are already weaving one variation when you use two colors. However, for all these first samples, we suggest using two strongly contrasting colors of the same yarn. This is to let you follow the exact path of the warp and weft, and see the structure of the weave.

Other looms and ways of using them follow in the next chapter, which is about student experiences. We did all our photographed examples for the series that follow on small cardboard looms

with taped and notched ends, five warps to the inch, and began weaving with one or two strips of cardboard and a few rows of plain weaving for a heading.

What will we weave?

First, we will weave an example of each of three basic weaves, to learn the ways of each one:

Plain Weave.   Basket Weave.   Twill Weave.

Then we will come back to each one and play with a number of ways to change it. You will have a chance to use your own design and color ideas.

Plain weave characteristics

It *does* look plain! Yarn just quietly going over and under, making the simplest structure, the most commonly used. It is the weave you see in shirts, blouses, sheets, pillow cases, and most other household textiles. One weft yarn goes over and under one warp yarn at a time, the same as in darning. When there are exactly the same number of threads per inch of cloth in both the warp and the weft, and both are of the same weight yarn, the weave is properly called "tabby." However, in usage, the term tabby is often used interchangeably with the term plain weave, and means the same thing.

Basket weave characteristics

It does remind you somewhat of baskets, as we showed you in the chapter on baskets. It is related to the plain weave, except that two weft yarns together are woven over two warp yarns at a time.

Twill weave characteristics

This weave is easy to recognize because the direction of weave is diagonal — on a slant instead of parallel to the warp and weft as in plain and basket weaves. You will learn by weaving it, that while the row of weaving is straight, the slant is made up of stair-steps of yarn as it crosses the warp, over two and under two. This happens because each row of weft is stepped up and over a new pair of warps.

Twill weave is commonly used in jeans, wool suitings, and sport-jacket tweeds. It is a little more complex than the first two weaves, but you can even do it the slow way, with a needle, on a little loom, just to learn where the yarns go. If you want yardage, this is one of the weaves that really must be done on a loom with heddles and beater and treadles. It requires four changes of the shed to complete the pattern unit.

You will need

• Cardboard, quite firm and stiff. The backs of sturdy writing tablets are good, or poster board.
• Tape for ends. We used Scotch strapping tape, a reinforced tape made for use on packages. Masking tape is also a good choice.
• Warp and Weft. Cotton/rayon medium-size rug yarn, two contrasting colors. (We used Aunt Lydia's, Art. 235.)

• Tapestry needles, two or more.
• Two strips of cardboard about 1/4-inch wide and an inch longer than the width of the warp, to use at beginning and/or end.
• Scissors, ruler, pencil, fork or comb for beater.
• Glue. Elmer's or similar quick-drying, colorless glue to secure ends of weaving.

MAKING THE LOOM

Figures 4-1, 2, 3, 4. Fasten a piece of tape across the top and bottom (the short ends of the cardboard) lapping it over like a binding. You may need to use more than one strip. Two layers of strapping tape on ours kept the ends from bending, and our loom lasted for several warpings.

Mark every 1/4-inch across the top and bottom. Be careful to have the top row exactly opposite the bottom row so your warp will be straight. In these first samplings, it is best to have space between each warp for easier weaving.
To notch or to slit, for holding the warp:

We tried both v'd notches and cutting a slit to hold the warp. With this large yarn, we found the notch was much more satisfactory, whether the loom was warped on one side or warped all the way around (figure 4-3). Slits are best when you use a smaller warp yarn like cotton carpet warp or string. We like the idea of warping both sides at once, and then weaving a sample on each side. This works out, even when your design calls for two colors in the warp. We just wove two verions. With heavy yarn, there is less strain on the notches when warping around than when taking it from notch to notch on the top side only.

WARPING

Use the yarn right from the skein without cutting into lengths. Put a knot in the end of the yarn, slide it down into the first notch. Wind it around and around the cardboard, putting it through each notch, top and bottom. Pull firmly as you go. Keep the tension as even as possible, but do not stretch the yarn. Secure at the last notch with a knot, or tape. If you want a crescent loom, cup the cardboard slightly as you warp (figure 4-4). This gives you a cradle-like loom with space underneath the warp providing a little more weaving room. Pins may be used to space the warp, as shown.

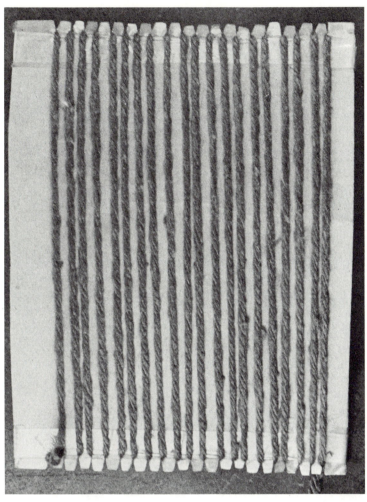

4-3. Cardboard loom with notches. This is the way we made our loom for most of our small samples. (Photograph by Mike Buckley.)

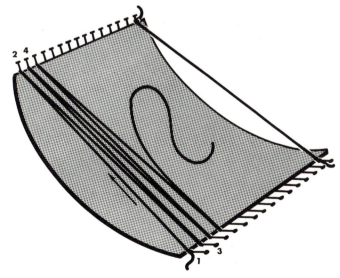

4-4. Crescent loom. Warp your loom so it bows slightly, for a loom with more working space under the warp. Teachers have found this works out better with some young weavers than using the loom flat. (Drawing by Virginia von Phul.)

HOW TO BEGIN THE WEAVE

All samples are begun in the same way, so these directions will not be repeated for each one.

Weave one strip of 1/4-inch cardboard into the warp, over and under. Push to the bottom of the loom as close to the notches as possible. This will help to even up the tension, and gives you a good base to weave against. You may want to weave in a second strip of cardboard, but usually one is enough. On these small looms it is easiest to use a tapestry needle for a shuttle. Thread the needle with weft yarn, several times longer than the width of the warp. This heavy yarn will be used up in a hurry. Even though it is awkward for the first few rows, it is a good idea to use a long length so you won't need to keep joining in a new weft end. Refer to "General Hints," page 66.

NOW — *FINALLY* — LET'S WEAVE

The author has prepared 24 samples to guide you, numbered for your convenience. You may want to number your own sampler file in the same way, so you can readily refer to the weaving directions in this book at a future time.

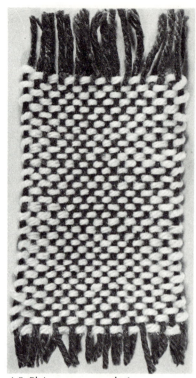

4-5. Plain weave, sample 1.

4-6. Basket weave, sample 2.

1. Plain weave

Warp your loom with one color.
Weft: The same kind of yarn used for the warp, but a contrasting color.
Weave over one and under one, back and forth. Press or beat down each row of weaving with comb, fork, or fingers, so the rows just touch each other. The warp will show. Refer to page 67 for advice on how to keep the weaving even and not drawn in at the sides, by employing "bubbling," to keep the weft yarn relaxed.
This is plain weave (figure 4-5).

2. Basket weave

Warp your loom with one color.
Weft: The same kind of yarn used for warp, but a contrasting color.
The double weft yarns should not be twisted, but lie flat, one next to the other. On such a small sample, you can use your weft yarn doubled if you wish, and straighten it out if it twists. Or weave each weft separately, one at a time in the same

4-7. Twill weave, sample 3.

row. Weave over two warps and under two warps the full width. Weave over and under alternate pairs of warps in the second row, and so on, just like plain weave. Press down each row until it just touches the row below, with double weft lying flat. (Figure 4-6.)

3. Twill weave

Warp your loom with one color.

Weft: The same kind of yarn used for warp, but a contrasting color.

Thread a single weft yarn in your needle. Start at the right side of your loom. Four rows of weaving, stepping over and up on five warps, complete one pattern unit. The diagonal will go up to the right. Study the photograph of this weave (figure 4-7) and you will see where the yarn goes. There will be a single warp at the edge of every other row, which must be caught in, but the sequence of the weave is over two and under two.

Row 1. Right to left: Under first two warps, then over two, under two, and so on for the width.
Row 2. Left to right: Over warp one, then under two, over two and so on for the width.
Row 3. Right to left: Over two, under two, and so on for the width.
Row 4. Left to right: Under one, over two, under two, and so on.

Follow this sequence. You will see the diagonal begin to appear. Just remember: in each row, step to the next warp — one of the pair woven in the row before. You are weaving a little stairway.

VARIATIONS ON THE THREE BASIC WEAVES

And now for the fun of weaving some changes and additions to the basic weaves. We tried most of these mentioned and had them photographed for you by Kent Kammerer. But use them for inspiration only — use your own design ideas for your samples.

You can weave: Dots, spots, slits, stripes up, stripes across, plaids, bars, tufts, loops, knots, bumps, holes, borders, circles, blobs, knobs and lumps, diagonals, lines, squares, diamonds. Cloth that is thick, thin, sheer enough to see through, open warp, furry, smooth, bumpy, or combinations of any of these.

Spots: Scatter them, or arrange in rows like dotted stripes.
Bars: Like a broken stripe, uneven spacing for interest.
Stripes: Choose a pretty combination of colors, have some wide, some narrow, some just a line. Width between stripes, showing the background color, is important, too. Vary the colors, the size of the yarn, and use nubby yarns with smooth.
Check or squares: Single lines, blocks of color. Put loops or tufts in the center of some.
Plaids: Thick and thin lines, both warp and weft. Zigzags, herringbone, diamond twills. And more!

Here are ideas to explore, and samples to make as you learn how the warp and weft work together to make patterns, creating variations to see how the yarn moves in and out of the warp.

PLAIN WEAVE VARIATIONS

Plain weave can be changed in countless ways. Some weavers spend a lifetime weaving nothing but plain weave, and always create something that looks new and different. A plain weave is the best foundation for yarns added on the surface. When you put in heavier wefts, plain weave surrounds or supports it. Plain weave is a good background for applied or woven-in patterns. As a background, it can be inconspicuous or it can be the whole exciting design itself.

True tapestry is a plain weave, with the variation of a completely covered warp, and the introduction of many colors and patterns; colors are joined in different ways at any point. These variations of a plain weave give tapestries their own unique style — a whole set of different techniques.

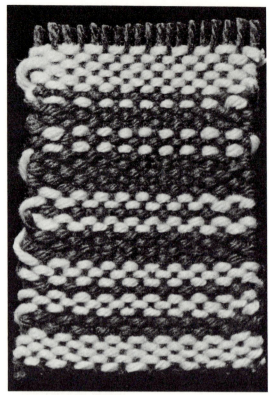

4-9. Weft stripes, sample 5.

4-8. Wide and narrow stripes, sample 4.

4. Wide and narrow stripes (figure 4-8)

Warp your loom with two colors. Arrange the warp in stripes of different widths. Design a stripe that is an interesting combination of widths — not exactly the same width in all of the stripes.
Weft: Plain weave, one color. The colors in the warp will appear as stripes. Beat in each row of weft so it just touches the row before, letting the warp show.

5. Weft stripes (figure 4-9)

Warp your loom with one color.
Weft: Two colors. Plain weave. Weave stripes of different widths for a pleasing effect.

4-10. Checks, sample 6.

7. Single line checks (figure 4-11)

Warp your loom in two colors. Decide what size you want your divisions. In our sample, we put one contrasting warp about every inch.
Weft: Same two colors as the warp. Plain weave, with one line of contrasting color to mark off each division.

4-11. Single-line checks, sample 7.

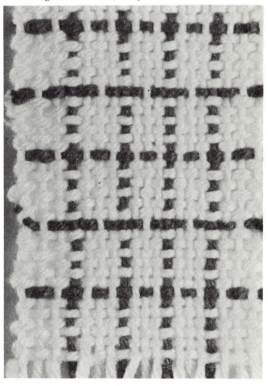

6. Checks (figure 4-10)

Warp your loom with two colors. Decide what size you want your squares. We made ours about 3/4 inch, warping alternate colors in 3/4 -inch stripes.
Weft: The same two colors as the warp. Weave plain weave in alternate stripes the same width as the warp stripes. The result will be squares of each color. Beat so the weft just touches the row before, and squares up the checks. If you want a true square, measure, because the exact number of warp and weft yarns may not weave to an exact square, and you may have to use one or two more, or less. You may want to lengthen the squares into rectangles by adding extra rows.

8. Alternating colors in warp and weft to make tiny checks (figure 4-12)

Warp your loom with two colors, alternating.
Weft: Try different effects by weaving with just one of the colors, by alternating rows of the two colors, and by weaving with just the other color. Weave a striped pattern, or all with just one color for a miniature check effect.

9. Plaids (figure 4-13)

Play with spaces and sizes of yarn. We used our same light and dark yarns and added a heavier black one. Use all three in both warp and weft. You can draw a plaid on paper, or work out the crossings and spacings right on the loom. On our little sample we have picked out a few spots that are especially interesting and for weaving a plaid fabric we would repeat some of these spacings and colors for our all-over pattern.

We like the little white-framed black square that turned up in the top row of black yarn. By counting the rows of weaving, and noting where the colors come in warp and weft, this little motif can be planned in. Here is a very good example of the design value of doing these little samples. At the right, about two-thirds down, between two rows of black, a little white flower motif appears. This, too, would be a good little pattern to repeat. Have fun with the plaid sample — make more than one.

4-12. Tiny checks, sample 8.

4-13. Plaids, sample 9.

10. Spots (figure 4-14)

Warp your loom with one color.

Weft: Begin the plain weave with the same color as the warp. This is your background. Weave in spots of the other color. See our little example for ideas. We used several sizes of dots and scattered them. Try dots, lines, flowers — some in rows, some at random.

Small dot: Weave over one warp. Push cut ends through to the back. Let hang about half an inch long so they won't pull out. If you want a lot of dots all in one row, weave over a single warp, then skip underneath and come up again over another single warp, and so on, for the width. Leave about half an inch of yarn hanging at each end of the pattern weft, on the back of the weaving. Weave a few rows of the background color, and do another row of spots or just one here and there.

For a line spot, weave over and under two or three warps, leaving cut ends at the back as you did for the dots. Make a thicker line or spot by weaving a double pattern weft.

For a flower-like spot, weave over one warp, as you did for a dot. Weave background color. In the next row, weave over and under three warps above the dot. Weave background color. In the next row, weave over the same warp as the first dot. A flower!

Continue with rows of background plain weave. Flowers can be made larger by weaving over the same warps for two rows each time. Play around with this idea, and make a meadow full of flowers!

4-14. Spots, sample 10.

4-15. Overshot and float, sample 11.

11. Overshot and Float weave (figure 4-15)

Overshot and Float weave describe exactly what happens in this pattern weave. Some of the yarns float over the background tabby weave, so the design is woven against a plain weave. Many of the traditional pattern weaves — Colonial coverlets, for instance, use variations of this. Such large pieces, of course, must be woven on a large loom with the pattern threaded in. But we can have some fun with them and learn a lot with our small samples, just to see what the possibilities are.

Float weaves require more rows per inch of weaving to make a really firm background for the looser wefts which lie over the background. These patterns are useful in almost any kind of wearable or household fabric. The pattern must be thoughtfully designed for use. A long overshot on upholstery would not be practical because it would be caught and pulled up. A very long overshot on the reverse side should be used only when the material is to be lined or backed up as in upholstery. The exception to the rule: For a purely decorative fabric, where a firm structure is not too important, a spongy, loose weave with long overshot is acceptable — and can be a stunning part of a design.

For our little sample, we will weave a good background of plain weave along with the overshot rows. You will find that the tabby rows pack in. The long floats ride over the background. A delightful· design element to experiment with. Here is how you do it.

Warp your loom with one color. Look at our example for ideas on how to place the overshot rows, but use your own design.

Weft: Two colors — one the same as the warp, and a contrasting one. Weave over and under with the pattern weft, sometimes on single warps, sometimes skipping over four or five in a giant step, then under two, over two, and so on. Always weave at least one row of plain weave background between overshot rows, beating in firmly, so the warp is well covered.

For another variation: Proceeding very carefully, so you won't cut the background, slide the tip of your scissors under some of the longest floats and cut them in the center. This will give you some fluffy cut ends to add to the interest and texture of the weaving. These float-cut areas can be arranged on your plain weave background in rows or groups. Leave some long floats uncut for a still different effect. This pattern weave is great fun to play with, and a useful one for small weavings, because you can create an interesting surface with little effort. Notice how the background recedes and the pattern stands out. The way the lights and darks are placed has a lot to do with the look of it, too. Even if you use the same color for background and pattern, you will have a fabric with surface design and texture.

Two names that have been given to this cut-float weave are "bangtail" and "eyelash." Spotted in an otherwise plain textile, it is one more way to make a simple weave sparkle with your own individual touch.

12. Loops (figure 4-16)

Loops are made by pulling the weft up around a gauge to raise the weft above the plain weave background. (See figure 4-30 for how to do it.) Loops can be put in rows, blocks, lines, or as single dots. You can make geometric designs and borders or emphasize small units of a woven pattern by raising loops as an outline or a solid pattern.

Warp your loom with one color.

Weft: Two colors, one the same as the warp. Each row of loops must have a row or more of plain weave in between, to help anchor them. The plain weave must be beaten in very firmly, otherwise the loops will pull out easily. They lie on the surface, and depend upon a very tight background to hold them. Pulled up loops like this are practical, even for rugs, when woven on a large loom with fine yarn as a firm background.

Design an arrangement of squares and rows, then enjoy lifting your design from the background into loops; we used a knitting needle to pick up the loops. If you prefer, you can use all one color. We put contrasting colors in the background, too, to add the rows of flower-like pattern. You can make your loops various sizes or all the same size! you can make some flat, some really loopy.

As you see, there is an almost endless parade of things you can do to enrich a plain weave background and give it the special look of being hand-woven. Design a large wall-hanging combining several of the variations you have learned, using many colors and many sizes and kinds of yarn.

4-17. Random basket weaves, sample 13.

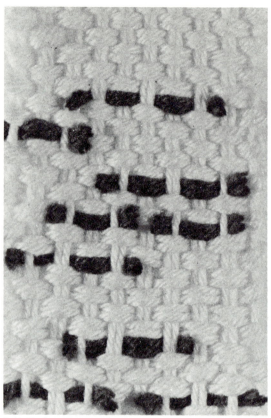

4-18. Basket weave with bars, sample 14.

BASKET WEAVE VARIATIONS

In a true basket weave, a number of wefts cross an equal number of warps, usually two and two. Change the look of it by weaving over four warps with four wefts, or three and three, in all one color, or contrasting.

13. Random basket weave (figure 4-17)

Warp your loom with one color.
Weft: Weave in contrasting color, basket weave, but change the number of warps and wefts in a random weave across each row. Do the same thing using only one color, the same as the warp. Some good examples of this are in Chapter Five.

14. Basket weave, two and two, with bars (figure 4-18)

Warp your loom with one color.
Weft: Weave two-and-two basket weave with the same color as the warp. Weave in short lengths of another color. Leave cut ends on top surface to add texture.

Change the effect with color, by warping with pairs of different colors. Then use more than one color in the weft. You can weave a regular checked basket weave with two colors in warp and two colors in the weft. You can arrive at quite a complicated plaid by different sizes of yarns, several colors, along with changing numbers of warps and wefts woven together. Most of the variations of plain weave can be woven on a basket weave background. These hints for variety in this weave should keep you busy for awhile!

TWILL WEAVE VARIATIONS

15. Zigzag twill (figure 4-19)

The slope of the diagonal lines is slightly different in the two parts of our example, where the direction of the slant reverses. In the bottom one, two wefts are put in row five. This deepens and widens the points. In the upper one, the slant changes in row five with a single weft. This makes the zigzag narrower.

Warp your loom with one color.

Weft: Contrasting color. Weave the first four rows as you did for the basic twill. Then reverse the slant as follows:

Row 5. Right to left: Over warp one, then under one, over two, under two and so on for width.

Row 6. Left to right: Over warp one, then under two, over two, and so on for width.

Continue the sequence for the four pattern rows. Change directions again, and weave the same as the first four rows.

16. Diamond twill (figure 4-20)

We wove a slight change in the two diamonds; a small change in one row of weaving makes the center flowers slightly different. In Row 6, of the diamond at the top, weave under two and over two for the whole width. This makes the center motif look a little more like a flower.

Warp your loom with one color.

Weft: Contrasting color.

Row 1. Right to left: Under first warp, over two, under two and so on for width.

Row 2. Left to right: Under two, over two, and so on for width.

Row 3. Right to left: Under two, over two, under two, over two, under four, over two, under two and so on until end of row.

Row 4. Left to right: Over two and under two, the whole width.

Row 5. Right to left: Over two, under two, over two, under three, over two, under three, over two and under two.

Row 6. Left to right: Under two, over two, under three, over one, under two, over one, under three, over two, under two.

This is the center of the diamond, and the rest of the rows are the same, only in reverse, reading up from row five. Weave a few rows of twill in the background color, then weave another diamond.

Note: In other chapters you will see examples of variations of these weaves as well as herringbone and other twills.

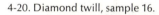

4-19. Zigzag twill, sample 15.

4-20. Diamond twill, sample 16.

4-21. Plain weave tapestry, sample 17a.

4-22. Plain weave tapestry, sample 17b.

PLAIN WEAVE TAPESTRY

Another way to put designs in cloth is by tapestry weaving. This can be woven as a complete pictorial design or spot designs can be put in. Pictures and patterns are put in by hand — the weaver, instead of the loom, controls the design. Heddles are not required, especially on small tapestries, but are of help where large areas of plain weave are a part of the design. Slits, slanting lines, circles, geometric designs, and modeled, curving lines are all possible, using the appropriate techniques of joining and returning colors and building up areas of pattern.

Tapestry designs are the same on both sides, because the weft yarn is not carried from selvedge to selvedge as in regular fabric weaving. The warp does not show; the weft is pushed down firmly to cover it, and colors are joined and returned. Wool is the traditional, and the most satisfactory, yarn for tapestry weaving. It is soft, covers the warp completely and beautifully, blends into itself, and the colors are unlimited.

TAPESTRY TECHNIQUES

True tapestry weaving requires skill, experience, and design ability. Basic methods to learn are the ways of joining colors at the color change-point, blending colors for subtle effects, and fine detail. In *Weaving is for Anyone* we made a study of tapestry weaving, with working drawings of the various methods of covering the warp, blending colors, and a suggested sampler of techniques. We refer you to that for deeper study of tapestry weaving. For a start, it is helpful to make a large-scale sampler, so you can continue your sampling with the same rug yarn. We used the same cotton/rayon yarn for ours, so you can see quite clearly what happens to the yarn. If you wish to do a tapestry with a more detailed design, you will have to use a finer warp and weft, set at about eight to the inch.

17. Tapestry samples

Two samples in the same techniques. One (figure 4-21) is not beaten down to cover the warp, as it should be in a tapestry, therefore the yarn path can be followed a little more easily. The other (figure 4-22) is beaten in so the warp is covered as it should be in a proper tapestry.

Warp your loom with one color.

Weft: Two colors, alternating from side to side, so each separate method can be clearly seen.

Slit. Plain weave from edge to the center, around the warp and back again, for ten or twelve rows. With the other color, weave back and forth from the other side to the center, leaving an opening, or slit.

Dovetail joining. Switching colors to the opposite sides, weave in from one edge to the center warp, around it, and back again. Now, with the other color, weave in from the other edge to the *same* center warp, around it and back to the edge. Repeat, alternating from side to side, always taking the alternate colors around the same center warp. You can see the joinings like clasped fingers. Weave ten or twelve rows. For the next rows do the same dovetail method, having switched colors to opposite sides again. This time take each color around the common center warp two times before changing color. You will see that this joining becomes quite noticeable and decorative, with a zigzag line like rickrack.

Interlock joining. Switch color sides again, and weave a few rows with interlocked joining method. Weave each color in from each side in the same shed. At the center, *between* warps, bring the two wefts around each other and return. On the sample that has been beaten in tightly (figure 4-22), you will notice that there is no uneven line, but the joining is straight and smooth. Weave some rows with interlock joining.

Weaving on a slant. Again change sides with the two colors and begin to weave the white triangular shape at the right. Weave in to the center warp, around the warp and back. Then in to the center again, but this time bring the weft around the next warp to the right, and back to the edge. Continue to weave rows in this way, each time stepping over one warp, until you have done the triangle, and have gone around and back on each warp, out to the edge. Now go back and begin weaving the dark shape on the left. Weave back and forth, covering all of the warp, going around each warp and following the slanting line of the white weaving. When you have woven about eight or nine rows, weave all the way up the side of the white triangle to the edge, around the outside warp and back down the slant, continuing across to the left hand edge. This is one way to outline a shape.

Continue the dark weaving over and back to the center, making a slant, in reverse, like the other. Then, with the white yarn, weave back and forth in the small triangle of warp left unwoven. Weave a few rows all the way back and forth at the top. Finish with a few rows of dark yarn. You can make two of these samples, one with warp showing just to learn the ways, and one with the warp beaten down properly, or you can do the solid one only. Samples 18, 19, 20, and 21 are all variations of these techniques: the slit, modeling, and weaving on a slant. (See figure 4-23.)

4-23. We did the tapestry techniques with big yarn on a very widely spaced warp so you can follow the path of the yarn for each technique. From the bottom up: Slit. Interlock joining of colors. Dovetail (single). Weaving on a slant. (Photograph by Kent Kammerer.)

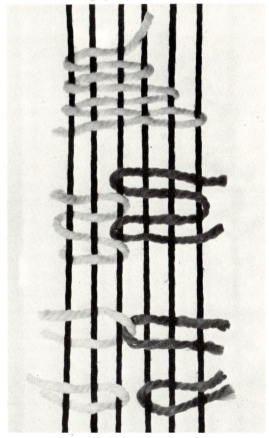

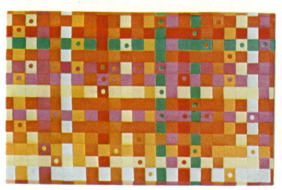

Top left
C-2. An example of really early weaving. This is a reconstruction of a Stone Age fence on the Island of Jutland, Denmark. (See Chapter 2, "From Source to Woven Baskets.") Rough-hewn posts interlaced with branches. Plain weave! (Photograph by Gary Wilson.)

Bottom left
C-4. Paper weaving. Cut strips, some perforated. Weaver, Lowell Hanson. University of Washington class work. Teacher, Richard Proctor. (Photograph, Audio Visual Services, University of Washington.)

Top right
C-3. Tapestry woven by Sandy L. Wakeman, age 12. Seventh grade, John Marshall Junior High School, Seattle. Designed after hearing African myth read by her art teacher, Mrs. Roberta Barnhart.

Bottom right
C-5. Circus Wagon. Detail of tapestry woven by Lois Fink in the Albany Adult Education Class, California. Teacher, Louaine Collier Elke.

18. Modeling and blending (figure 4-24)

Warp your loom with one color. In this technique the warp will be completely covered. With two colors, weave a small composition of ovals or a circle, or a diamond, as shown, and short and long curving lines. By weaving over a few warps, back and forth, and increasing by one or two warps at a time, you weave the shapes. Modeling is a combination of this and actually pushing the weft around where you want it! You can press it down with a fork to follow a curve or weave lines on a slant. Just try it and see how it works.

19. Slits and angles (figure 4-25)

Warp your loom with one color.
Weft: Weave with two colors, alternating sides. Weave back and forth from each side, leaving a slit, and forming angled shapes, weaving as you did in the first sampler, but this time make a simple composition.

4-24. Modeling and blending, sample 18.

4-25. Slits and angles, sample 19.

4-26. Squares, slits, tufts, sample 20.

4-27. Open warp and slit, sample 21.

20. Squares, slits, and tufts (figure 4-26)

Warp your loom with one color.
Weft: Weave with two colors. Weave back and forth just as you did when you made the slit-weave sample, only make smaller areas divided into squares and oblongs. Change colors to make a kind of checkerboard. Add some loops where the colors change, and put a loop or knotted tuft in the center of some.

21. Open warp and slit-weave (figure 4-27)

Warp your loom with two colors.
Weft: Weave with two colors. Weave areas as you did in sample 20, but leave some of the warp unwoven. Design the space with dark and light areas balanced in a good composition with the woven and unwoven warp.

Opposite
C-6, 7. Two bright sun symbols. Plain weave tapestry, using slit weave as a design element. Tiny — only about three- by three-and-one-half inches — they have been slightly enlarged here to show details. Woven of very fine yarn, with a knowing use of color and technique. Weaver, Jane Hopkins. (Photographs by Kent Kammerer.)

4-28. Woven raised design.

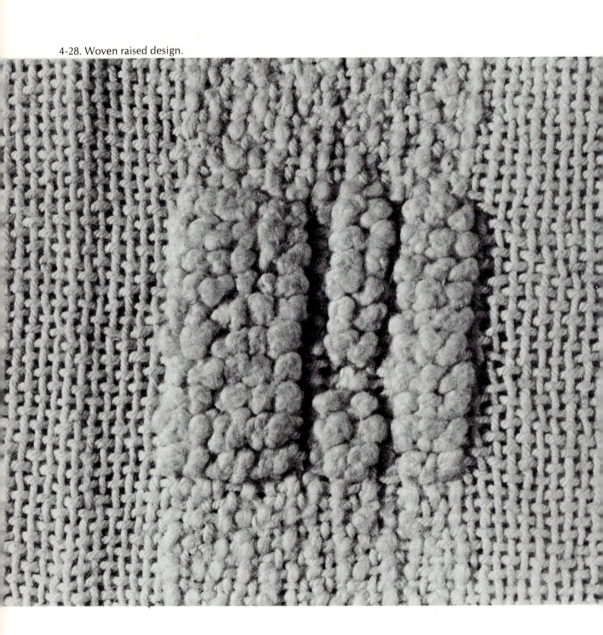

MORE WAYS TO ENRICH A PLAIN WEAVE TEXTILE

Once you become a weaver, you will find many more ways than we can mention here to add interest and texture to an otherwise plain material. These are the things that add spice to the designing and weaving. Most of the suggestions below are quite simple, and as you become more expert, you will invent more. A series of samples experimenting with some of these ideas will add a great deal to your weaving study file. Give your weaving a one-of-a-kind handwoven look. That is part of the reason for hand weaving — to do something that a machine cannot do.

• Combine several of the plain weave variations in one fabric. For example, use two warp colors; weave horizontal stripes with two weft colors; change from rows of plain weave to basket weave, floats, twill, and back to plain weave; use multiple wefts in some rows.
• In a plain warp stripe, weave tapestry squares at random within the width of some of the stripes.
• Pick out small units of pattern in the weave and emphasize them with added color or heavier yarn. Lay in while weaving, or add later with a needle.
• Plain weave rows woven in a certain way with contrasting color will appear as rows of chain, little flowers, toothed bands, depending on the color change.
• Use loops or knots to emphasize pattern areas or make design motifs. Weave a set of monogrammed napkins along this idea in plain weave with smooth yarn, a band woven in with matching nub-spun yarn (figures 4-28, 29). The initial was raised into loops. Placemats and a tablecloth to go with these napkins were woven on the same cotton warp: the weft was all plain weave in the textured yarn. This made a quiet but rich background for dishes and food, with the design motif only on the napkins. (See figure 4-30 for how to pick up loops.)

4-29. Raised monogram.

4-30. If you follow the path of the big yarn on the widely spaced warp, you will see how to pick up loops, make the Ghiordes Knot, singly, with several yarns in one, and with continuous yarn, over a gauge.

4-31. Example of Ghiordes Knot left in loops, sample 22. Also see examples in Chapter 5.

GHIORDES KNOTS

22. Ghiordes Knots are the traditional way of weaving pile rugs. This way of putting in pile or texture is shown in a large-scale how-to-do-it fashion, in figure 4-30. They can be left in loops, or cut, packed into a solid pile fabric, or used as a line or area. The fifth-graders at Mountview Elementary School had a wonderful time with them, and used them to good effect. (See Chapter 5.)

Warp your loom with one color. For our sample (figure 4-31) we used just one color weft. We made our knots over a gauge and left them in uncut loops. In some rows we did a little flat weave, making a design of flat and looped pile. (Photograph by Mike Buckley.)

DEVELOPING BORDER DESIGNS

23. Warp a loom with two sections of warp — black for one side, and white for the other. Then play with different weaves — plain, basket, multiple wefts in one shed — alternating black and white to get different pattern effects. Weave all the way across with rows of black, then with white, and see what a different look occurs in each side. Weave some all on the white warp, with black weft, and at the same time weave the black side with a white weft. Use the slit weave technique. The sampler shown in figure 4-32 was woven by the author. (Photograph by Kent Kammerer.)

EXPERIMENT WITH THREE-DIMENSIONAL EFFECTS

24. Do a row of slits, using several yarns and colors (figure 4-33). Ours are yellow, browns, and orange — wool, linen, and cotton ratine. Weave wires in along the edges of each woven strip, like an extra warp. We happened to have some of the plastic-coated copper wire used in electrical installations, a red-orange, but any wire will do, depending upon how stiff you want it. Pipe cleaners would work, too. Bend the strips any shape you wish. This idea was inspired by a long memory of the paper lanterns we learned to make in kindergarten! Woven by the author. (Photograph by Kent Kammerer.)

4-33. Three-dimensional effect, sample 24.

4-32. Border designs sampler, 23.

Student Experiences

To make sure that the sampling ideas in the previous chapter were valid and would really be of help, I talked to many teachers, camp counselors, weavers, and non-weavers. Their suggestions and help were welcome and useful. Several teachers used a draft of the sampling chapter in their classes. Information on paper weaving is included in the present chapter, since many teachers felt it was the best way for children to start. Class experiences in weaving are given in detail, from the efforts of seven-year-olds at camp through art teachers' studies at university summer schools.

PAPER WEAVING

Paper weaving is accepted as a useful introduction to teaching the basic principles of weaving. Teachers have found that very young children can manage wide paper strips more easily than they can manage yarn, when they first try weaving, and in addition, paper weaving is useful as a design tool on all grade levels. A pattern can be designed and woven in paper, with easy change of colors and interlacement, as a study for a weaving project.

Paper weaving in itself is a fascinating craft. If you do paper weaving for it s own sake, you may well end up with a selection of good designs to translate into yarn. Our photographed examples represent a cross-section of age groups, from elementary school to teachers; they were chosen to show that paper weaving, even when done at an early age, is not just measured straight strips put together in plain weave. We think they are all really exciting, and should give you lots of ideas. Many of the sample textile weaves given in Chapter 4 could be done in paper.

Opposite
5-1. Designing with paper. Development of a border design, using the cut-out pieces to echo the shapes of the void. By the author. (Photograph by Kent Kammerer.)

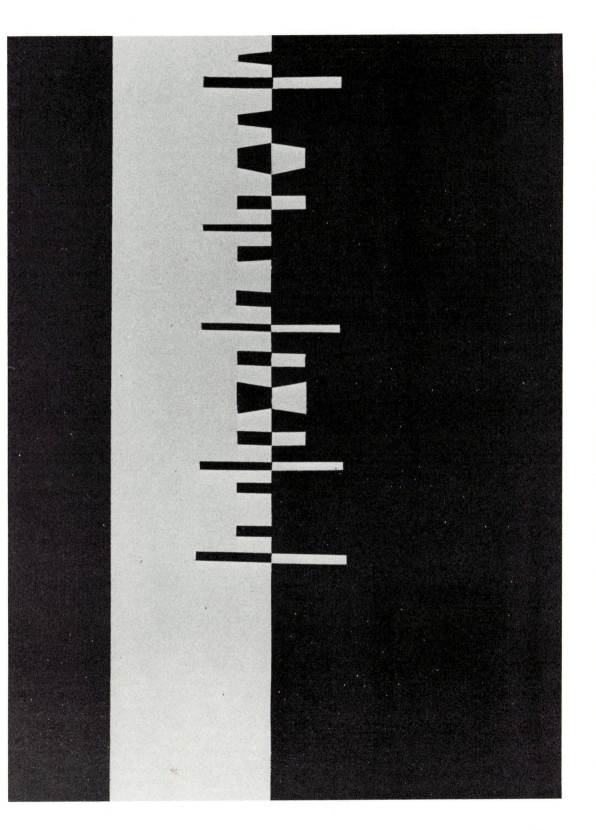

5-2. Paper weaving. Cut paper, two colors. Lorrie Bisconer, age 8.

Below: 5-3. Paper weaving. Left, Lorna Zeiler, age 8. Right, James Sand, age 8. Figures 5-2, 3, third grade, Cascade School, Renton, Washington. Teacher, Mrs. Gruber. (Photographs by Kent Kammerer.)

Try some of these

All the following, and more, can be done in paper weaving:

• Straight strips in one direction, shaped strips woven through.
• Both warp and weft strips can be cut into curving, angular, and diagonal strips.
• Extra strips of other colors can be woven in over wide strips.
• Colored tissue paper in layers can build up colors, and you may find a brand new color!
• Small areas of added pattern shapes can be pasted on.
• The paper weaving on Color Page 84 uses perforations for added dimension and pattern.

Designing with paper

Making a design cartoon for rug or tapestry weaving with cut or torn paper is fun. Experiment with tissue paper; it is available in a complete range of

beautiful and subtle colors. Tear or cut strips, place them in different positions and colorways — the overlays will create in-between colors, and this comes close to the color relationships that occur in weaving. Moving the papers about is fun, is quick, and gives you lots of combinations of pattern and color.

Another way to design a rug is by using torn strips of construction paper to arrive at a pleasant pattern and color arrangement. The fuzzy, torn edges simulate the uneven edges of wool pile. You can overlap, layer, and move the colors and shapes around like a puzzle. These materials and methods are all exciting design-makers.

A DESIGN STUDY

The Seattle Weavers' Guild members, with the late Jane Givan Johnston, did a series of studies on designing for the loom. During this study, we used cut and torn papers. Black and white papers and

5-4. Design study in cut paper and the woven piece. Left, cut paper; right, pattern translated into weaving. A raised loop technique in chenille yarn on a flat background weave was chosen, suggested by the torn paper pattern shown on the following page. The pattern was somewhat changed and simplified in the weaving.

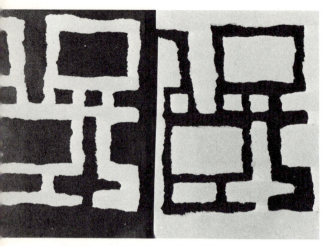

5-5. The same design as figure 5-4, done in torn paper and carried out in two ways, black on white and white on black, to better study the composition of light and dark. By the author. (Photographs by Kent Kammerer.)

Weave: Over one, under one — plain weave. Ends are folded back and pasted down. Woven by David Smith, age 11. (Figure 5-6.)

2. Begun the same as 1., but two weft colors are used. All weft rows have the two colors in the same shed. Plain weave. Woven by Nonda Kelley, age 13. (Figure 5-7.)

3. Warp paper folded the width, cut in a definite symmetrical pattern. The middle cuts are widest, and become narrower toward the outside. Weft is all the same width. Simple one over one weave. A framing paper, cut in an irregular jagged pattern, frames and covers the ends. This one comes and goes right off the page! The cut frame adds a nice finish, and another dimension to the pattern. Woven by Dan Thomas, age 13. (Figure 5-8.)

4. Random groups of slits were cut into the background paper, and various colors were woven through them. The lightest colors do not show in the black-and-white photographs, but we liked the idea of the open pattern. It achieves a nice freedom and a departure from the rigid paper squares and strips. Woven by Gary Garrett, age 13. (Figure 5-9.)

yarns are best to observe the relationships of pattern and space. The steps to be followed in one assignment were:

• Draw over a grid, arranging the space into rectangles and squares.

• Make changes until a well-balanced pattern is achieved.

• Use cut black and white paper to see how pattern works. Rearrange as necessary for a good design.

• Do the same pattern in torn paper. White on black, then black on white.

• Weave your design.

Studies of this kind are very helpful. If you are pleased with one, consider it a thumbnail sketch for a real weaving project.

FOUR PAPER-WEAVING PROJECTS

Classroom paper-weaving projects, shown in sequence. Teacher, Richard Dye, Federal Way, Washington. (Photographs by Richard Dye.)

1. The background paper (warp) is folded in half, lengthwise, and random cuts are made to within an inch of the edge. Weft: even width strips, torn.

WEAVING ON CARDBOARD LOOMS BY FIFTH GRADERS

A long, delightful afternoon was spent with about 30 young weavers, aged 10 to 11, at the Mountview Elementary School, Burien, Washington. Their teacher, Tom Reeder, had really stimulated their interest in weaving, and they were eager and busy. They were shown examples of very good weaving of all kinds. Using *Weaving is for Anyone* (Van Nostrand Reinhold) he had taught them how to do the Ghiordes Knot, Interlock, and Dovetail tapestry techniques for joining colors; plain weave, and the use of the slit and open warp. Following a draft of our preceding chapter, they wove some samples — Plain, Basket, and Twill weaves. Then they elected to take these apart to conserve the yarn — and to get going on wallhangings! It was interesting to observe them at work. In a group this large, interest and talent naturally varied a great deal. Some of the children wove more than one piece and still had ideas left over. Others did the required minimum, using the simplest of designs. A few did some extra pieces at home.

5-6. Random-cut paper weaving (1).
5-7. Paper weaving with two weft colors (2).

5-8. Interesting symmetrical paper weaving (3).
5-9. Open-pattern paper weaving in various colors (4).

5-10. This weaving, very well-done, was left on the loom to show the kind of chipboard and pin loom used in the class at Mountview Elementary School. Background stripes of white, lemon yellow, and yellow-green. Rows of white Ghiordes Knot loops. The loops are not packed in, so they fall airily over the stripes. Weaver, Lori Elder, age 10. Teacher, Tom Reeder, fifth grade, Mountview Elementary School, Seattle. (Photograph by Kent Kammerer.)

Mr. Reeder chose chipboard, 1/8 inch thick for the looms. This is much more rigid than cardboard and will stand hard use and re-warping. It is flexible enough to make a crescent loom, which is done by drawing the warp just tight enough to bow the loom a little and give more weaving room below the warp. (See figure 4-4.) Some of the weavers here did this. Chipboard comes in sheets 38 x 27 inches, so six looms were cut from one sheet, each 9 x 19 inches. This is a workable size for use with heavy cotton yarns, and will produce a piece of weaving about 8 by 16 inches. Weavings varied in size a great deal, according to the design, yarn, and the time and interest of the weaver.

Chipboard is too tough to cut into notches without special tools, so pins were the best solution to hold the warp. No. 3 straight pins were used. They are longer than the ordinary common pin used for sewing, and are made of a stronger metal. Two layers of masking tape were put on like a binding over the top and bottom edges of the loom for added strength. Chipboard is thick enough to allow the pins go in quite far, and they can be hit sharply to drive them firmly into place. These looms really took a lot of rugged use, including stacking on a table between weaving classes. Many survived several warpings.

Warp: White string or cotton carpet yarn.

Wefts: Weft yarns were mostly the large, soft cotton rug roving and medium size cotton/rayon rug yarn, with some smaller amounts of wool worsted and some novelty yarns. The color range was wide and glorious, as you can see from our color photographs on page 103.

Designs. Using colored crayons, each student made a cartoon of the design he wanted to weave, which was taped to the loom, under the warp.

Techniques. Plain weave, interlock, dovetail, and slits were the most-used techniques. Ghiordes knot loops — which they loved — were put in for texture. Color choice, technique, and design were the weaver's, with guidance from Mr. Reeder.

Results. The results were so good with these first-time weavers that it was difficult to select only a few to show in our limited space. The youngsters were thrilled to have their work considered for a book, and each child provided me with a card giving a description of the yarn and design.

I suspect this experience was more rewarding for me than for anyone!

5-11. Fifth-grade weaving on cardboard looms.

Figure 5-11, left to right:

A very long weaving for a first piece, done on a cardboard loom; the tendency to draw the weft in and then relax the weaving and widen it again adds to the design, almost as if the shaping were planned. Spots of tapestry weave in several colors are woven on a white background. Some areas are joined, some leave slits. A row of Ghiordes Knot loops finishes the top and bottom edges. Weaver, Diana Paul, age 10, who wrote: "I have loops. It's a big loom."

Three small, flat weavings show use of loops, stripes, and angled shapes woven with large cotton rug roving, with interesting use of color.

Weavers, Ken Laviola, Mario Scott, Leta Plummer, all age 10.

Three little seamless handbags woven on cardboard looms. Handles are braided strips, sewn on later. All were woven in one piece, like a pocket, over and around the loom. The two striped ones are of large cotton rug yarn. Top, right, three purples, black, blue, gold, and pink stripes. Weaver, Leta Plummer, age 10. Bottom right, stripes in greens and white. Weaver, Virginia Noyes, age 10. The all-white bag, right center, is made of small-size cotton/rayon rug yarn, left with warp ends hanging to add a decorative screen of fringe. Weaver, Dawn Cramer, age 10. (Photograph by William Eng.)

5-12. Weavings with rug roving.

Figure 5-12:

Three pieces, all woven with large rug roving.

Joanna Hill, age 10, wrote: "Background: Aqua. Shape: Black dog with white ear."

Mario Scott, age 10. "It is a ship in the ocean and has two smoke stacks and two clouds in the sky."

Jeff Moosman, age 10. "It had no loops. Its background is blue. Its pattern is triangle. In one triangle is a man." Jeff was intrigued by the small figures in a Guatamalan weaving, and tried to make one. He learned that small, detailed designs must be done with fine yarns and not the large cotton roving.

(Photograph by Kent Kammerer.) See Color Page 103 for more weavings by this class.

TAPESTRIES BY SEVENTH GRADERS

A seventh grade elective art class, under the imaginative direction of Mrs. Roberta Barnhart, art teacher at John Marshall Junior High, Seattle, Washington, wove some handsome tapestries. Mrs. Barnhart gave them a very good foundation in design and color; stirred their imaginations by reading legends from Africa and about the Pacific Northwest Indians; provided them with an exciting collection of colorful wool yarns; taught them one tapestry technique — Egyptian Knot, selected from *Weaving is for Anyone*, and the results are first weavings of remarkably good craftsmanship and design. Each student was responsible for obtaining his own frame loom. Some of the looms were put together by the student, or with help at

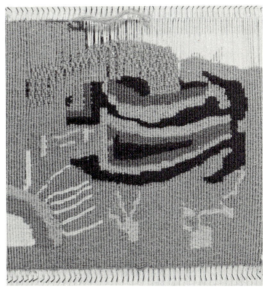

Above left
5-13. Mask. Shades of red and gold, Egyptian Knot tapestry technique. Woven by Cynthia J. Olney, seventh grade, John Marshall Junior High, Seattle. Teacher, Mrs. Roberta Barnhart. (Photograph by Kent Kammerer.)

Below left
5-14. Mask, inspired by a Pacific Northwest Indian legend. Woven by Mary Ann Gojenola, seventh grade, John Marshall Junior High, Seattle. Teacher, Mrs. Roberta Barnhart. (Photograph by Kent Kammerer.)

Above right
5-15. Legend of the Sun and the Whale. Karin Krueger wanted a "watery-look" in part of the background, so after seeing various tapestry techniques, she did some warp-wrapping. Shown on her small frame loom. Seventh grade, John Marshall Junior High School, Seattle. Teacher, Mrs. Roberta Barnhart. (Photograph by Kent Kammerer.)

home. Most were about 15 inches square. The warps were large seine twine or cotton cord. The wefts were wool knitting worsted.

After removal from the looms, some were mounted on burlap of a blending color, stretched around wood or cardboard for stiffness. Some were sewed to a felt background, with a hem at the top, a dowel with wooden ball ends, and a braided cord for a hanger.

The author visited the class and showed them some other weaving techniques when they were about halfway through. Some of them added another stitch or outlining for a variety of texture. The experience was rewarding for everyone. Some of the children want to go on to other weaving and more tapestries, some are satisfied with just the one, but all felt it was a pleasure. And all of them earned a top grade! (See Color Page opposite.)

Below left
5-16. Whale and Thunderbird legend. Note the skeleton fish inside the whale! Weaver, Cathy Cross, seventh grade, John Marshall Junior High School, Seattle. Teacher, Mrs. Roberta Barnhart. (Photograph by Kent Kammerer.)

Below right
5-17. The Whale. Woven in rich, warm tones from pink through orange to red-purple, with black outlines, this tapestry suggests stained glass. Weaver, Todd Bell, seventh grade, John Marshall Junior High School, Seattle. Teacher, Mrs. Roberta Barnhart. (Photograph by Kent Kammerer.)

Opposite
Seven "first" weavings by fifth graders in the class of Tom Reeder, at the Mountview Elementary School, Seattle. (Photographs by Kent Kammerer.)

C-8. Top left. Woven by Jeff Moosman, age 10: "It has no loops. Its pattern is a boat and sun and water." Bottom, left to right. Mike van Dyke, age 10: "I have on my weaving different colored loops and they are in a triangular shape." Don Impson, age 10: "It is covered with loops of different colors." Don used two sizes of yarn, and eight colors. Scotty Crandell, age 11: An abstract design made by drawing random lines, then filling in spaces with colored crayon. Plain weave tapestry, dovetail joinings.

C-9. Right to left. Dawn Cramer, age 10. The simplicity of two colors on white, a diamond and triangles, loops for texture make a very effective small wall hanging. Lori Elder, age 10, says it all in her note: "All colors. Pattern: squares. No background." This is a good use of open warp as a part of the over-all design. Lori Brewer, age 10: Beautifully simple — just rows of white and colors, with the ends fluffed. Lori wrote: "Colored stripes, fussy ends, no loops."

C-10. Design inspired by the story of a Monster who swallowed a knife. Interesting use of color in blocks of diamond shapes. Outlining in orange wool, chainstitch, added after the tapestry was woven. Mounted neatly on black felt. A dowel with round ball ends is slipped through the top hem, a chainstitched cord is the hanger. Weaver, Ron Bullock, seventh grade, John Marshall Junior High School, Seattle. Teacher, Mrs. Roberta Barnhart. (Photograph by Kent Kammerer.)

C-8.

C-9.

C-10.

WEAVING IN HIGH SCHOOL

Two belts woven by senior students at Renton High School, Renton, Washington. The wide sash is beautifully woven in two colors of wool, bright blue and light, bright green. Woven on a small four-harness table loom, with beater and reed. The warp pattern stripe is different on each side. Ends are simply finished by a row of knots and warp fringe. Weaver, Diana Leonhardt. Teacher, Mrs. Dorothy Stickney. (Photograph by William Eng.)

The narrow belt was woven on an inkle belt loom. The arrangement of black warps along the edges creates a patterned edge. The center is light brown and green. Ends are knotted into three small tassels, with all the center warps pulled together and the few outside pattern warps tied into a shorter fringe. Weaver, Karen Finnicum. Teacher, Mrs. Dorothy Stickney. (Photograph by William Eng.)

5-18. Two belts woven by high school students.

COLLEGE TEXTILE DESIGN CLASS

Larry Metcalf, Assistant Professor of Art at Seattle Pacific College, Seattle, Washington, conduc weaving classes for art teachers in the summe quarter. The teacher-students learn beginnir weaving, textile design, and weaver-controlle techniques, using small looms. Their use of card board, stick, and frame looms is original and points out another way to do three-dimensional and free-form weaving. All the different weaves are explored: plain, twill, basket, tapestry, color joinings and slits, wound warp, soumak, chaining and twining. These are fascinating studies of texture, design, color and form. Woven by art teachers, under the imaginative direction of an artist-weaver-teacher, the results are really fresh and inspiring.

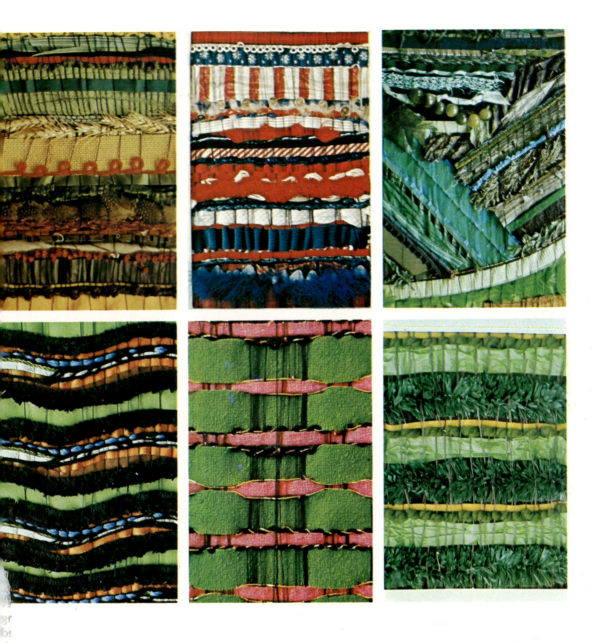

C-11, 12, 13, 14, 15, 16. A study for the development of textiles. Textural patterns in non-repeat and repeat: top row, non-repeat of pattern; bottom row, repeat of pattern. Seeds, beads, bark, lace, paper, leaves, stems, cloth, and open warp, all on a very fine black warp, set wide apart. Student work. Teacher, Larry Metcalf, Assistant Professor, Art Department, Seattle Pacific College, Seattle. (Photographs by Larry Metcalf.)

DEVELOPMENT OF TEXTILE STRUCTURES

Three assignments: Flat weaves. Leno (lace) constructions. Free-form weaving.

Flat weaves

To begin with, the teacher-students develop textile structures in a manner much like our sampling idea. The assignment then requires them to make a pillow, using three different yarns, all wool, all the same color. A planned part of the problem is to design the closing, deciding whether it is to be a concealed zipper, a decorative stitch, or inconspicuous. A flat, chipboard purse loom is used.

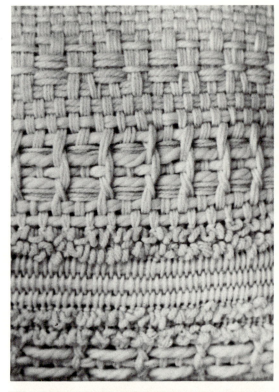

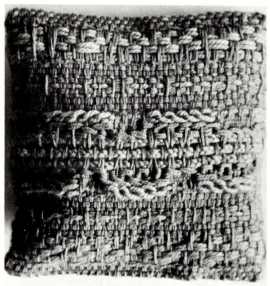

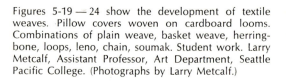

Figures 5-19 — 24 show the development of textile weaves. Pillow covers woven on cardboard looms. Combinations of plain weave, basket weave, herringbone, loops, leno, chain, soumak. Student work. Larry Metcalf, Assistant Professor, Art Department, Seattle Pacific College. (Photographs by Larry Metcalf.)

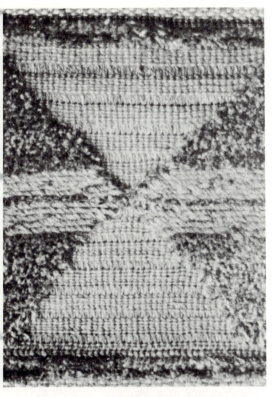

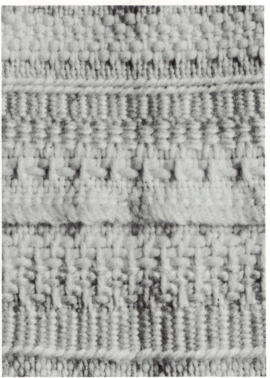

5-25. Cardboard strip beating device.

5-26. Cardboard strip on edge forms shed.

The loom

The purse loom is just like our sampling cardboard loom, warped all the way around. It is about 12 inches square. For the pillow, weaving continues all the way around, making a pocket, open on one side.

A simple shedding and beating device is shown in figures 5-25, 26. A strip of stiff cardboard picks up warp threads, in pattern, across the full width of the loom; a ruler or smooth strip of wood can be used. It is turned on edge to form a shed, used flat to act as the beater, and is removed to pick up pattern warp and make the next pattern shed. The weft yarn is put into butterflies or wound on a stick shuttle. On a small project, the weft can just be threaded into a long tapestry needle. (See flat weave examples, figures 5-19 — 24.)

LENO (LACE) CONSTRUCTIONS

Leno is an open weave in which warp yarns are twisted between rows of filling. The crossed warps keep the filling or woven wefts from slipping or moving out of place, making large open spaces possible. Crochet cotton, hard twist linen, or seine twine are good choices for experiments with this technique. The problem here: To weave interesting areas surrounding equally interesting open spaces. Textures are added with loops, knots, multi-wefts, chainstitch, and braided wefts. (Figures 5-27, 28.)

Figures 5-27—33 all show student work. Teacher, Larry Metcalf, Assistant Professor, Art Department, Seattle Pacific College, Seattle. (Photographs by Larry Metcalf.)

5-27. Leno construction.

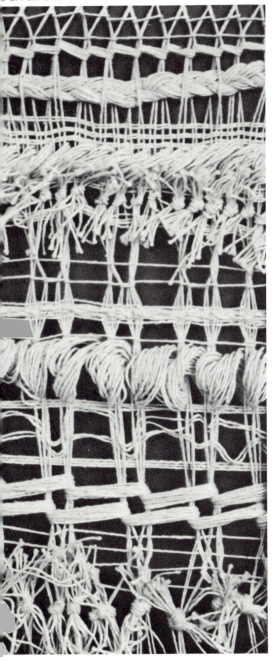

5-28. Leno construction.

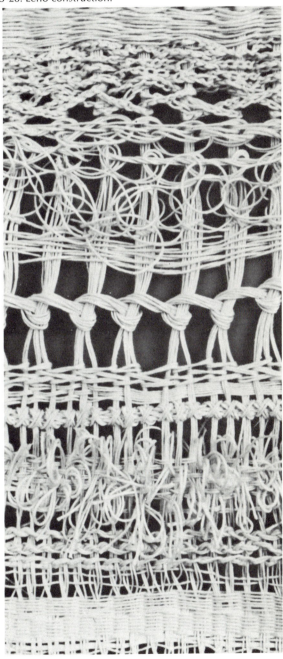

5-29. Warp fastened to dowel.

5-30. Curved branch used as warp beam.

FREE-FORM WEAVING

Free-form, three-dimensional, anything-goes weavings were done on combination stick and cardboard looms.

The loom

The warp is fastened to a branch, stick, or dowel, which serves as the top or warp beam, and also as the hanger when the wall hanging is finished (figure 5-29). Sometimes the natural curve of a stick or branch chosen sets the line of weaving, and more branches may be added to the pattern (figure 5-30). The stick, or branch, is then mounted on a slab of Styrofoam, a little larger than the planned weaving. This is dense Styrofoam with a smooth surface — the kind used in floats and toys for swimming, and for light weight picnic coolers. The loose end of the warp is secured to the Styrofoam with pins, tied completely around, or held fast with tape. This arrangement allows the weaver to manipulate loose ends of warp into braids, twists, macramé sinnets, or whatever suits the fancy. Weaving is usually done from the top down, but can be done from either direction. After some weaving has been finished, supplemental cardboard looms can be added (figures 5-30 — 32). These permit the weaver to weave a pocket, like the pillow or a purse, which is later stuffed and sewn together, to create another dimension. The weaving can be split and go off into separate "legs" that can be any shape. Unlimited effects are possible. Sometimes the loom is left in to stiffen the weaving. Top warp ends can be knotted, wound, braided, tasseled, or woven into tabs. Warp ends at the bottom can be finished decoratively also, in any of the techniques, adding beads, dried material, or feathers. There were no restrictions on color, material, or techniques used in this assignment.

Design discipline

Please note, however, that no matter how uninhibited, free weavings need thoughtful planning and a certain discipline if they are to come off as good designs. Without planned relationships of color, shapes, textures, and over-all form, they can turn out to be just a confused mess! See Color Page 124 for reproductions with details of some of these free-wheeling-designed weavings.

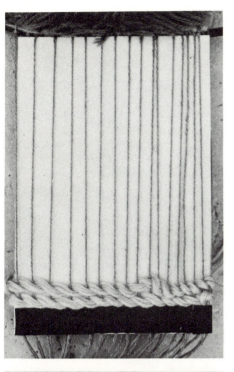

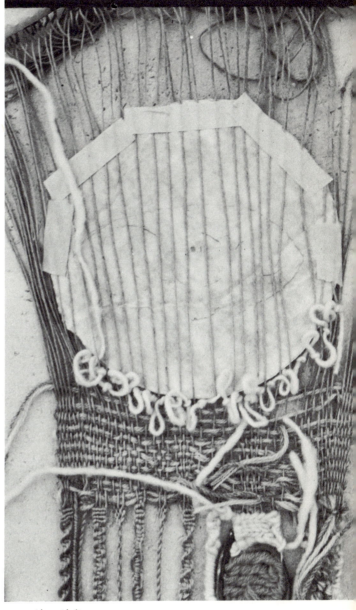

Above left
5-31. Added cardboard loom (which just shows at lower right in figure 5-30). Tape has been put across the bottom to hold the warp, and two rows of twining have been started at the bottom.

Below left
5-32. Loom added to weaving at bottom left, just visible in figure 5-30.

Above
5-33. A round shape taped to the warp as a means of weaving Ghiordes Knots and loops in a circle.

5-34. Tapestry weave. Woven strips on extra warps overlay the background. Top award winner in the 1969 Northwest Craftsman Exhibition, Henry Gallery, University of Washington. Weaver, Betsey Bess. (Photograph, Audio Visual Services, University of Washington.)

5-35. Small tapestry showing modeling and hatching. Student work. Teacher, Betsey Bess, University of Washington. (Photograph, Audio Visual Services, University of Washington.)

MORE ABOUT WEAVING CLASSES FOR TEACHERS

A summer arts and crafts class for teachers at the University of Washington developed some small weavings with good ideas and uses of tapestry techniques. The weaving was under the direction of Betsey Bess, whose own weaving is influenced by her two years in Peru working for the Peace Corps. A photograph of one of her tapestries, of alpaca yarn in natural colors, is shown in figure 5-34.

Looms and techniques

Most of the weaving in class was done on frame looms — picture frames, home-made frames, or canvas stretcher frames. Some used string heddles; some used smooth wood strips for making a shed. Plain tapestry weave with all of its variations of color change, modeling, hatching and blending were explored. Two bright little plain-weave tapestries from this class are pictured in figures 5-35, 36, and figure 5-37 depicts three sampler tapestries.

5-36. Tapestry. Weaver, Lowell Hanson. Teacher, Betsey Bess. (Photograph, Audio Visual Services, University of Washington.)

5-37. Sampler tapestries, exploring tapestry techniques. Student work. Teacher, Betsey Bess, University of Washington Art Department. Weavers, top down: Susan Duncan, Julie Blakemore, Ernest McClusky. (Photographs by William Eng.)

SUMMER CAMP PROJECTS

Weaving on simple looms is a favorite craft project in summer camps. At Camp Nor'wester on Lopez Island, Washington, they have some very talented and imaginative people as counselors. Artists and craftsmen, they provide a variety of projects for their little campers.

Under the direction of Marty Holm, a group of girls about seven to nine years old did some weaving on a variety of small simple looms. She reports that the backstrap (belt) loom was the favorite.

This is the hole and slot heddle loom, fastened to the waist of the weaver and to a solid object like a tree. It is fondly known to campers and counselors as the popstick or TD loom because it is made of popsicle sticks or tongue depressor sticks stapled together to make a heddle and shedding device (figures 5-38, 39, 40, 41). Campers used this loom to weave guitar straps and belts out of colorful cotton yarns. Surrounded by woods and fields, they also used natural materials, such as the inside bark of cedar trees, bracken fern stems, sheep wool caught on wild rosebushes, grasses, cattail stems and leaves.

5-38. Karen Holm, age 7, one of six little girls tied to backstrap looms attached to trees at Camp Nor'wester on Lopez Island, Washington. She is intent on weaving a belt, on her little popstick loom. (Photograph by Timothy M. Lamont.)

5-40. Dilynda Fischer, age 9, a fifth-grader from Anchorage, Alaska, weaving on a popstick loom at Camp Nor'-wester. (Photograph by Dick Weatherford.)

5-41. A simple, home-made heddle belt loom. Also called hole-and-slot heddle, or backstrap loom. Camp Nor'wester. Counselor, Marty Holm. (Photograph by Dick Weatherford.)

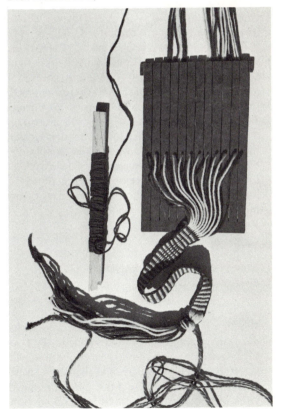

5-39. Monica Stack, age 9, a fourth-grader from Portland, Oregon, weaving a belt on a popstick backstrap loom, at Camp Nor'wester. Counselor, Marty Holm. (Photograph by Dick Weatherford.)

5-42. Floor loom for weaving mats.

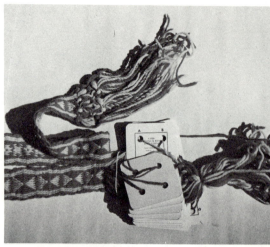

5-43. Card weaving.

An unusual floor loom was used to weave mats. The weaving frame is suspended on two uprights. A large spring coil is the warp spacer-heddle. The beater is a coarse comb with metal teeth set into a wooden frame. The weaver is Dilynda Fischer. (Photograph by Dick Weatherford.) (Figure 5-42.)

Cardweaving was also done at Camp Nor'-wester. A guitar strap is in the making here (figure 5-43). This is a way to weave very firm, good-looking straps and bands and belts. The cards are the loom, with perforations for 'yarn to go through. To make the pattern sheds, the cards are turned. Books have been written about this belt-weaving method; please consult our "List of Useful Reference Publications" on page 138. Cardweaving is fun for a family project on camping trips or at home, an ideal occupation for rainy days or evenings.

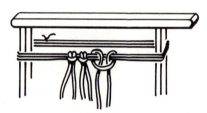

5-44. This is the top of a bag loom, used for twining bags. It shows how the holding warp is put around — you can put it around a shoe-box-lid loom in the same way — and how the free-hanging warps are attached. The twining rows are put in from the top down.

TWO EXTEMPORANEOUS LOOMS

Shoe-box-lid loom

The idea of using a shoe-box lid for a loom like the twining bag loom shown in figure 5-44 was suggested by Mrs. Raymond Marsh of Kennewick, Wash., to Mrs. Bert Yenney of Walla Walla, Wash., who showed a group of little girls about eight years old how to weave little bags on shoe-box lids. The top, or holding warp is fastened around the shoe box lid. Pairs of warps are fastened on with a half-hitch, ends hanging free. Starting at the top, rows of twining go round and round the lid. When the bag is the desired length, it is slipped off the loom. The bottom is closed by knotting the front and back warp ends together, leaving a fringe. The top edge is a finished selvedge formed by the warps put around the holding cord, and the rows of twining. (See Chapter 2, figure 2-2 for twining technique.) Handles were made and sewn on afterward. Mrs. Yenney made these two bags. They are exceptionally firm and very well done. The handle on the bag at the left is a sturdy braid made of three strands, each of which was first braided from three strands of the cotton rug yarn used in the bag. The other handle

5-45. Bags made on shoe-box-lid loom.

is braided with the same white and turquoise yarn as used for the bag. Weaver, Mrs. Bert Yenney. (Photograph by Kent Kammerer.)

5-46. Pencil loom.

Pencil loom

Patty Lou Reed, 10, proved that a loom is where you find it! She made a pencil frame loom, and wrote: "Tie each end of pencil with long pieces of yarn. Bring the other two ends together and attach to map holder at top of bulletin board. Tie each end of another pencil with long pieces of yarn and attach other end or anchor to a chair close by. Now, tie the warp threads. Weave with contrasting color of yarn." Richard Dye, teacher, Federal Way, Washington. (Photograph by Richard Dye.)

Weaving
IS Fun!

To demonstrate that weaving really *is* fun, here is an assemblage of weavings—whimsical—charming — childlike — imaginative — some for and some by children.

Part of the joy of weaving is making a design or pattern, not just plain cloth. One way to do this is by the tapestry method; directions for pictorial, or tapestry, weaving, and other exciting ways to accomplish interesting woven effects are well covered in Chapter 4, "Learning by Doing."

WAYS TO HAVE FUN WEAVING

• Weave around an object. For the core, use a cylinder of cardboard, a dowel, driftwood, a large stone, carpenter's scraps in interesting shapes. Weave a cage around a shell, a rock, or a sturdy leaf.
• Weave a pocket for a dress or sweater.
• Do a strap for your guitar, or a tote basket.
• Make a colorful belt or headband.
• This is the year of the scarf, so weave a colorful one of fine wool.
• Weave a background, and apply shells, leaves, tiny driftwood, Christmas ornaments, straw shapes, or other found objects you have collected. Not too many in one weaving, of course — plan your composition and keep to a harmonious theme of color, texture, and applied objects.
• Weave a wall-hanging with a variety of grasses, leaves, branches, cones, or whatever treasures you find in woods, garden, or on the beach. Our garden is overrun with horsetails. This jointed grass loves a damp location such as that along our stream. Since we lost the fight to erase them — and they are quite handsome *outside* of the pebble terrace — they were woven into surprisingly good-looking sturdy mats and hangings. Exciting wefts are all around you, waiting for you to find them. (See figures 2-1 — 20 in Chapter 2.)

Here are weavings by boys, girls, men, and women, within a wide range of experience, training and talent, to show you what can be done.
• A whimsical little panel that has a good repeating pattern (figure 6-1). Small wooden cocktail forks alternate direction on a fine black warp. Bright blue, red, and dark green pipe cleaners in plain weave, fill the space between the forks. A strong, colorful band is created up the center. Weaver, Lowell Hanson. Teacher, Betsey Bess. (Photograph, Audio Visual Services, University of Washington.)
• This leaping creature, bumping his nose on the selvedge, is worked in a very small tapestry with lots of action packed into an eight-inch square! Woven on a small frame loom, it is almost a sampler of tapestry techniques — limning (outlining), slit, plain weave with interlocked joinings, hatching (blending), and modeling. (Figure 6-2.) Weaver, Kathy Packard. Teacher, Betsey Bess. (Photograph, Audio Visual Services, University of Washington.)

6-2. Small tapestry combines many techniques.

6-1. Repeat pattern: cocktail forks, pipe cleaners.

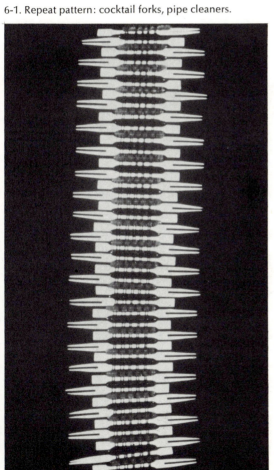

• Woven on a stick and Styrofoam slab loom with cardboard and pin looms added to weave the solid sections. (See figures 5-29 — 33 in Chapter 5.) Many colors and textures of yarn are used, mostly in plain weave, with some open warp and woven tabs at the bottom. White, black, gray, and orange predominate, with thick and thin spun yarns woven along with smooth ones. Student work. Teacher, Larry Metcalf, Assistant Professor of Art, Seattle Pacific College. (Photograph by Larry Metcalf.)

• Titled "Thread Patterns" by the weaver, this small wall-hanging is woven on warps of many layers. Open warp over woven areas, meandering threads over other warps and weaving, all finished off with a simple knotted fringe (6-4). Weaver, Laurie Herrick, Portland, Oregon. (Photograph, Audio Visual Services, University of Washington.)

6-3. A weaving on stick and slab loom.

6-4. Layered wall hanging.

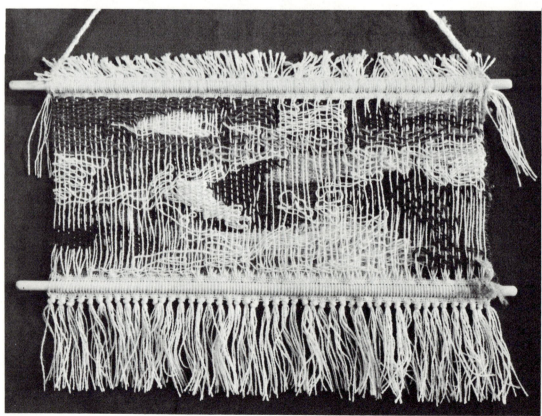

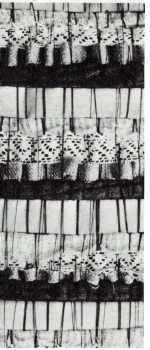

Left: 6-5. Black warp with lace stripes. *Center:* 6-6. Mementos of a wedding. *Right:* 6-7. White linen yarn Leno construction.

Design assignments

A serious design and weaving assignment, college level, can be fun, too! Below are three examples of three different design problems given to his beginning weaving class by Larry Metcalf, Assistant Professor of Art at Seattle Pacific College. Simple cardboard or frame looms were used. There were no restrictions on materials for the weft. Figures 6-5, 6, 7 show the results.

Problem: Repetition of stripes.
Result: A weaving on a very fine black warp; rows of varying widths and different materials for weft, including white cotton lace, folded bands of wool fabric, patterned white cotton, and smooth, fine cotton fabric strips.

Problem: Stripes, non-repetition. Related weft materials.
Result: Mementoes of a wedding. Weft materials in white or silver on a fine black warp. Lace, net from the veil, silver gift ribbons, pearls, little white roses, strips cut from the wedding invitation — and even a row of rice, enclosed in plastic! Very imaginative, and an interesting study of textures and proportion.

Problem: Leno construction — a lace-weave. The same white linen yarn used for warp and weft. Small frame loom.
Result: Warps twisted in the Leno technique, areas of plain weave, open warp, loops, and braided weft, all add up to a well-balanced composition of closed and open space with the added dimension of texture. Student work, courtesy Larry Metcalf, Assistant professor of Art, Seattle Pacific College. (Photograph by Larry Metcalf.)

Set up a problem for yourself, giving yourself limitations of material and design, and see what you can do.

6-8. First weaving by a seven-year-old.

6-9. Free-form by an eight-year-old.

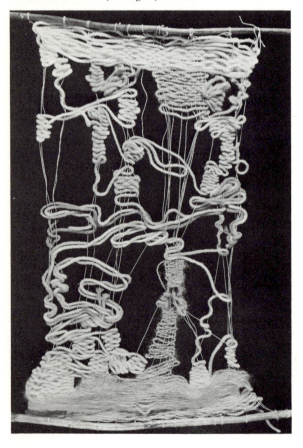

• A first attempt at weaving by a seven-year-old boy, all on his own, resulted in an interesting striped piece. He used a small cardboard loom, very fine cotton warp spaced about four to the inch. Light yellow and dark brown worsted is the weft. The two sizes of yarn make an undulating stripe, which is pleasantly repetitious. He had a casual approach to technique — cutting each row off at the selvedge, giving a cut fringe look at each edge. Weaver, Jerry Burns. (Photograph by Kent Kammerer.)

• Free, open wall hanging woven by an eight-year-old. It has a very fine mercerized cotton warp with wool wefts, knitting worsted, and a small amount of mohair, mostly in shades of pink and yellow with a little gray-green. Dry bracken fern stems at top and bottom. Woven by a student, Renton School, Renton, Washington. (Photograph by Kent Kammerer.)

• Feathers, branches, and wools, together with knowledgeable use of weaving techniques and design, produced this figure. The loom was a combination of the top stick, cardboard loom sections added, all mounted for working on a Styrofoam slab. (See Chapter 5.) Soumak, wound warp, plain weave, loops, double warps, and knots are all used to create the three-dimensional effect. Weaver, Larry Metcalf, Assistant Professor of Art, Seattle Pacific College. (Photograph by Larry Metcalf.)

• A request came to the State Capitol Museum at Olympia, Washington, for an exchange of folk-art between craftsmen in the State of Washington and craftsmen in Japan. The crafts were to be permanently housed in a museum in Japan. Weavings had to be rather small. Pondering on a possible subject for a miniature that would be interesting to people of another country, the author wove this little tapestry of faces. It is only about six by eight inches, and is sewn to a handwoven, textured cotton stretched over a piece of 1/8-inch plywood. (Photograph by Phil Davidson.) Also shown in color on page 65.

• Hands as a design element are endlessly fascinating to craftsmen. Perhaps because they are there! When you are Mary Hanson, a logical place to put woven hands is on a pocket. The weaving is in cotton, a Guatemalan pick-up weave, warp pattern. The top of the pocket is fringed; notice that the hands are in correct position. Weaver, Mary Hanson. (Photograph by William Eng.) For information on how to do this weave, and the weave

Left: 6-10. Three-dimensional free form. Right: 6-11.
Miniature tapestry. Faces. Below: 6-12. Guatamalan
pick-up weave.

123

C-17, C-18, C-19, C-20. Studies of textile development, using a stick for a top beam, employing different tapestry and knot techniques, and adding cardboard looms to weave pockets, which are stuffed for added depth of texture. Wound warp, plain weave, Ghiordes Knot, Leno, braiding, soumak, woven tabs and strips, as well as planned color areas. A detail is shown at right of each piece. Student work. Teacher, Larry Metcalf, Assistant Professor, Art Department, Seattle Pacific College, Seattle. (Photographs by Larry Metcalf.)

used for figures 6-13, see Shuttlecraft Guild Monograph Fifteen, 1965, *Guatemala Visited*, by Mary M. Atwater. Originally published in 1946.

• Weaving around objects is carried to a high degree of finesse in this imaginative wall-hanging. Nearly ceiling to floor in length, each strip is separate and all are hung from a heavy brass rod. Tin cans of many sizes and depths, some brass and some silver-color metal, have been pierced in a variety of designs. Each strip is double (tubular) weave, with layers separated to encircle a can, then woven back into a flat strip. Natural linen warp and weft enhance the soft sheen of the metal. Woven by designer-weaver Judy Thomas, who knows what she wants to weave and how to do it. (Photograph by Harold Tacker.)

• People are always interesting subjects for pictorial weaving. While we no longer need to weave carefully detailed tapestry portraits for posterity, man's instinct is to use real persons as models. Caught by a passing scene of little girls on swings, as she rode a city bus, Fritzi Oxley wove her little group of "Swingers." These completely captivating tots are woven of fine wool yarns in delicate pastels, on a fine linen warp. The airy, swingin' look is enhanced by the open warp, the complete separation of each swing, and by the device of hanging them from a thin brass rod set in a light frame. Done in plain weave tapestry with a few stitchery details added. Weaver, Fritzi Oxley, teacher of stitchery and weaving. (Photograph by Mr. Oxley.)

6-13. Weaving around tin cans.

6-14. LITTLE SWINGERS.

6-15. Alpaca yarn tapestry. Peruvian.

6-16. Detail of 6-15.

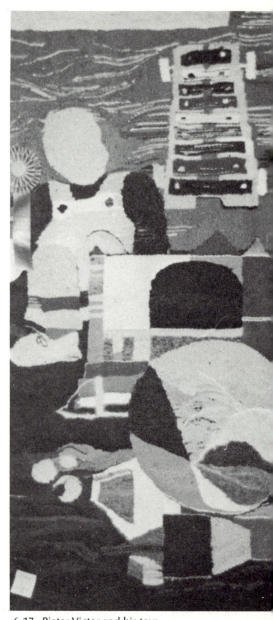

6-17. Pieter Victor and his toys.

● Two mask-like faces are woven into this tapestry wall-hanging from Peru, done in the natural browns, blacks, and whites of alpaca yarn. The whole piece was brushed to bring out the soft hairs of the yarn, making the right side of the material very soft and fluffy. A detail of the wrong side shows the plain weave tapestry with dovetail joinings. From the collection of Betsey Bess. (Photograph by Kent Kammerer.)

● A very talented textile designer and weaver from Holland, Marina Schut, wove this large tapestry depicting her small son, Victor, with his toys. Plain weave, modeled and blended, woven of her own handspun wools; some are dyed, but most are natural colors. The rosette at Victor's shoulder is not part of the woven scene — it is a best-in-show award ribbon by popular vote, at the Northwest Handweavers' Conference in Seattle. Courtesy Marina Schut, weaver — and Victor. (Photograph by Harold Tacker.)

● Another way to do a pictorial weaving is the painted warp or chiné method. The slightly blurred look you see occurs when the plain weaving goes over colors painted on the warp.

This technique can be done on any kind of loom. For a fairly clear design, the warp should be closely spaced. Keep in mind that your pattern will look slightly out of focus, and don't try for a crisp look; it is a good method to use when you want a blended, subtle look, and it can be combined with tapestry techniques and blended yarn colors for unusual effects. For the weaving here, raw silk yarn in a natural off-white was used for both warp and weft. The design, adapted from a Northwest Indian interpretation of an octopus, with his rows of suction cups, was painted on the warp with textile paints in a warm brown and dull orange. The top and bottom borders are brown and orange wool, with brown bracken fern stems woven in. Too subtle to show much in the photograph are random inlays of silk dyed with red earth from a bank along an Indian reservation.

A word about painting the warp: Be sure the paint is dry before starting to weave or to wind the warp through the reed and heddles. This piece was put on a four-harness floor loom, the warp tied in, then painted in front of the heddles. The warp was wound through onto the cloth beam, painted, allowed to dry, and then wound back, bringing it into place to begin the weaving. Woven by the author. (Photograph by Kent Kammerer.)

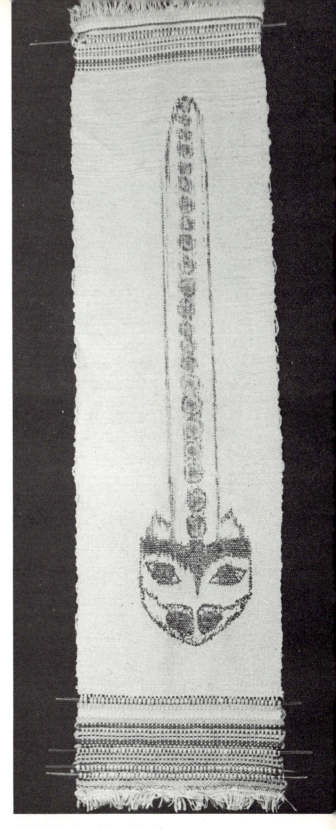

6-18. Painted warp pictorial weaving.

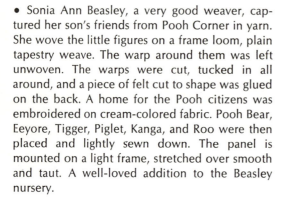

6-19. POOH CORNER. Nursery tapestry.

6-20. KANGA. Roo can be removed from pouch.

6-21. Ladybug woven on circle loom.

• Sonia Ann Beasley, a very good weaver, captured her son's friends from Pooh Corner in yarn. She wove the little figures on a frame loom, plain tapestry weave. The warp around them was left unwoven. The warps were cut, tucked in all around, and a piece of felt cut to shape was glued on the back. A home for the Pooh citizens was embroidered on cream-colored fabric. Pooh Bear, Eeyore, Tigger, Piglet, Kanga, and Roo were then placed and lightly sewn down. The panel is mounted on a light frame, stretched over smooth and taut. A well-loved addition to the Beasley nursery.

• We photographed Kanga by herself, so you could see her clearly. Roo is an entirely separate person, of course, and he can be taken out of his mother's pouch! Courtesy, the Dr. Palmer Beasley family. Weaver, Sonia Ann Beasley.

• A bright red Ladybug was woven on a circle loom in tapestry weave. Her legs are the warp yarns, braided. Backed with felt to keep her shape, she is moved about the Beasley home, making surprise appearances on a curtain, in the kitchen, or in the children's room — enjoyed by everyone. Weaver, Sonia Ann Beasley. (Photograph by Kent Kammerer.)

Woven birds

Birds are inspiration for weavers. Craftsmen in all media use bird forms. Historically, birds appear in textiles, paintings, architecture, sculpture; in stone, mosaics, and metal. Stylized, abstracted, or realistic, they provide a source of color, texture, and form that is unsurpassed. Here is a collection of birds, woven in a variety of techniques.

6-22. Pacific Northwest Indian thunderbird.

6-23. Mexican thunderbird.

• A classic Pacific Northwest Indian thunderbird design contrasts with a Mexican thunderbird. Both were woven recently. Both were designed from ancient and much-admired bird symbols. The pebbly texture of this wall-hanging was achieved by over-all weaving in Greek Soumak technique. Wool yarn, two ply and firmly spun, helps to create the large scale texture of the knot weave. The background is natural off-white. The bird is black, with soft blue and blue-green in the decorative spots. Note that the ends are prefectly finished with a braided warp fringe at the bottom. A row of braid finishes off the top. Weaver, Sonia Ann Beasley. (Photograph by Kent Kammerer.) (See *Weaving is·for Anyone* for how to do the Greek Soumak technique.)

• The Mexican thunderbird is plain weave tapestry, white on black, in soft, fine wool woven over a wool warp. This weaving is a very good example of the dovetail-joining tapestry technique, which results in a very effective broken line that adds much to the over-all design, especially when only black and white are used. The selvedge edge is firm and decorative in an elegant, quiet way. Both outside warps are made of several yarns, forming two heavy ridges when woven. The bottom edge is a simple fringe of warp ends twisted together in groups. Courtesy, Leslie McCune Hart, La Tienda, Seattle. (Photograph by William Eng.)

• A perky Mexican bird, black on a strong golden-yellow background. The dovetail joining makes a toothed edge that adds interest to the straight line representation. Soft, fine wool. Plain weave tapestry. From La Tienda, Seattle. (Photograph by William Eng.)

6-24. Mexican design. Plain weave tapestry.

6-25. Wall hanging from Ecuador.

• An exotic bird woven in Ecuador. Dark-red background sets off the white, green, and yellow creature. The wool yarn in the weft is very fine, but a little harsh. It is beaten in tightly over a fine white warp. The texture is crisp and firm, very good for a wall-hanging. From La Tienda, Seattle. (Photograph by William Eng.)

• Bird symbols in the hands of a Guatemalan weaver take on flourishes and furbelows. These haughty fellows march along the bottom edge of a woven and embroidered huipile (dress or blouse). Brilliant reds, green, yellow, and blue stranded cotton yarn. Collection of Leslie McCune Hart, La Tienda, Seattle. (Photograph by William Eng.)

• Superior-looking waterbirds, woven in wool, plain weave tapestry with dovetail and slit techniques. Woven by the author. (Photograph by William Eng.)

• This little owl, with his fuzzy baby features, is so appealing you want to pet him. His feathers are a soft olive-green mohair yarn. He is woven in Swedish Knot tapestry technique, and is altogether charming, standing in his deep frame. Courtesy of the weaver, Eugenia Duffy, student, adult weaving class. Teacher, Fritzi Oxley. (Photograph by Kent Kammerer.)

• A small, wise owl perches on a real branch, his feet curling around it for security. He represents a number of tapestry weaves, and an example of how a carefully chosen hanger can be part of the design. Plain weave tapestry. Swedish Knot, open warp, wound warp, and soumak. Warm golden and brown owl-color wools make up this winning little bird. Weaver, Sonia Ann Beasley. (Photograph by Kent Kammerer.)

6-26. Bird symbols from Guatemala.

6-27. Waterbirds. Dovetail and slit.

6-28. Baby owl. Swedish Knot technique.

6-29. A combination of tapestry techniques.

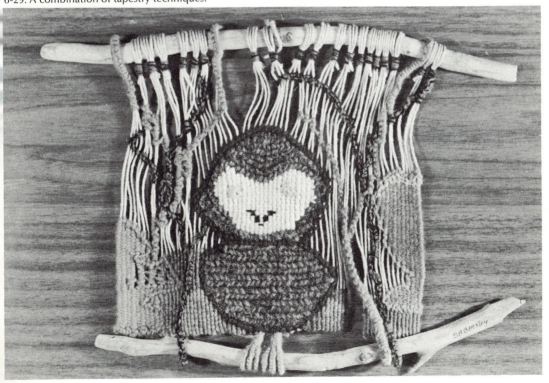

6-30. Simple and effective. Mexican.

6-31. Black sheep on white. Mexican.

6-32. Black frog on yellow. Mexican.

6-33. Raccoon in Swedish Knot technique.

6-34. Peruvian cat. Llama and alpaca yarns.

132

Animals

• Animals, too, are both traditional and modern subjects for craftsmen. Fanciful, charming animal figures are woven in wool by Mexican weavers today. Simple designs and strong colors, such as bright green or yellow, contrasting with black or white, were chosen for the three examples that follow. Planned for pillow tops, they are also effective as wall-hangings. Although there is minimum detail in the weaving, you can sense the agreeable feeling of the dog with a bird perched on his tail! Shown at left, opposite.

• A plump little black sheep ambles along against a white background.

• This black frog rests on a bright yellow base.

Above three, courtesy La Tienda, Seattle. (Photographs by William Eng.)

• Raccoons with their black robber masks are perfect subjects for a tapestry. This little one looks out from a background of forest camouflage, blended and modeled forms in shades of green, gold, and brown. Swedish Knot tapestry technique. Weaver, Lucile Chester, adult weaving class. Teacher, Fritzi Oxley. (Photographer, Kent Kammerer.)

• Peruvian cat. Plain weave tapestry of soft, fuzzy llama and alpaca yarns, woven in Peru. Natural colors, white, warm brown, and black, with just a touch of dyed orange yarn. The orange dye is obtained from a small Peruvian beetle. Collection of Betsey Bess. (Photograph by Kent Kammerer.)

Children

• Children, in a row, holding hands. A variation of a Guatemalan pick-up weave, warp pattern. Weaver, Mary Hanson. (Photograph by Kent Kammerer.) (See figure 6-12.)

6-35. A variation of Guatemalan pick-up weave.

6-36. Laid-in Guatemalan weave.

6-37. THE GIRL ON THE BAMBOO SWING.
Woven mobile.

6-38. Green wool, gold cord, silver rickrack.

• Birds and little people, a laid-in Guatemalan weave of very fine cotton warp and weft background. Pattern weft is stranded cotton. Collection of the author. (Photograph by Kent Kammerer.)

• "The Girl on the Bamboo Swing," woven mobile. Double weave, some parts stuffed, wound warp, tapestry weave, knotted fringe warps. She's pink and white and happy! Woven by Peggy Lavinder for her daughter's room, Puyallup, Washington. (Photograph by Kent Kammerer.)

Gay braids by five-year-olds

• Two little girls, whose mother is a weaver, made these bright braids to wrap special Christmas gifts. Left, by Maren Beck, age 5: Warp is green wool, fine gold cord, and wide silver rickrack; weft is red wool. Right, by Randi Beck, age 7: Warp is red pearl cotton, fine gold cord, narrow gold rickrack; weft, red rayon/cotton rug yarn. Fun for a family project, and can be done by the small fry with some help along the way. Courtesy, Ruth Beck and daughters. (Photograph by Kent Kammerer.)

6-39. Memories of Ireland.

IRELAND

• To capture the textures and beautiful colors of Ireland, on a three month holiday touring the country, the author wove several small "thumbnail sketch" tapestries (figure 6-39). These are being used as inspiration for larger works. Right: This one, in a dozen greens, is the springboard for a larger one, to be named "Forty Shades of Green," an Irish song title. Left: A St. Brigid's Cross, the legendary cross woven of river rushes, was fastened to a plain weave tapestry woven for it, in two shades of brown. Slits and thin lines of soft gold and orange echo the vertical lines.

• Irish houses, constructed on simple lines and painted every color in the spectrum, are also great subjects for a composition. (See the color reproduction of the author's tapestry "Irish Houses" on the back jacket of this book.) Sometimes a big, elegant idea for weaving has to wait for a better time, but quick little weavings help you hold the thought and are fun in themselves. (Photographs by Kent Kammerer.)

We think the examples in this chapter and throughout the book prove our point — that Weaving *is* Fun, and that anything goes! Often a playful woven piece, where you doodle and try different effects, is just a jumping off place for a larger and more thoughtfully designed weaving. You will find it is very true that the more you sample and weave and work with yarns, the faster the ideas will tumble. So, consult our sampling chapter, look at these weavings, then let yourself go — and *weave!*

6-40. IRISH HOUSES. Tapestry by the author. Another version is shown in color on the back jacket of this book.

TO SUM IT ALL UP

There are many, many more ways to weave cloth and tapestries than could possibly be even touched on in this book. Our intention here is to give you some idea of what weaving is all about, of just what happens when you put weft over warp in certain ways. We hope these samplings will help you to recognize different types of fabrics and understand how they are created. We hope you will have gained an increased interest in textiles, a greater understanding of the design and craftsmanship that goes into the production of any fabric and the many skills involved in preparing the raw materials — all the way back to a tiny silkworm, a fluffy sheep, or field of flax. Many of you will be interested enough to find out about the use of larger looms and different yarns. Weaving is a big subject; there are so many ways to do it, so many different kinds of equipment, so many kinds of weaving materials, such an incredible variety of cloth. All of us on this earth use textiles and baskets in some way in our day to day lives; we hope you have learned something about how they come into being. Animal, vegetable or man-made, fibers must be put through essential processes before they can end up as a piece of cloth for garments to wear, cloth to walk upon, or sit upon, or cover us at night — or to bring us joy as a lovely picture-fabric to hang on our wall. Best of all is the pleasure of learning a craft, and creating something worthwhile and beautiful.

Have fun!

Jean Wilson
February, 1970

6-41. CAPRICORN. Woven by the author, who is one. Tapestry of Icelandic mountain-sheep yarn and Wilson handspun. (Photograph by Kent Kammerer.)

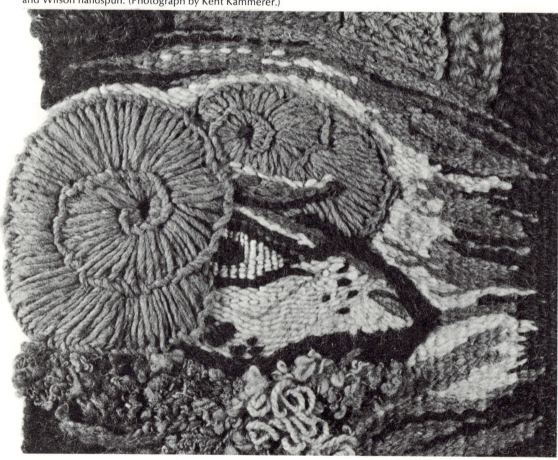

GLOSSARY

Arc (Bubbling) — Curving or slanting the weft in the shed so it will be relaxed and not pull in at the sides when beaten.

Beater — Device to move the weft down into place against the weaving. Can be a comb, fork, fingers, or warp stick. On a loom with heddles, it is the movable frame that holds the reed.

Bobbin — Length of weft wound and inserted into shuttle. Also butterfly or hand-bobbin.

Ends — Single warp threads. Warp ends.

Fiber — Filaments, natural or synthetic. Wool, silk, etc., as taken from the source, before it is processed.

Harness — Frame that holds the heddles.

Heading — Beginning rows of weaving. The first few rows are "throw-away" yarns or strips of cardboard to help even up warp spacing. The next rows act as a warp protection when cut off, and/or as a hem.

Heddles — String or metal devices with an eye through which the warp ends are threaded. Suspended in the heddle frame.

Loom — A frame to hold warp ends in tension. A device on which to weave.

Loom-controlled patterns — Those that are threaded through the heddles in a certain order, raised and lowered by the treadles. Cloth is woven in a loom-controlled pattern. Examples: twill, diamond, honeycomb, etc.

Pile Weave — Weft raised above the ground fabric. Looped or cut.

Plain Weave (Tabby) — The most simple of weaves — over one warp and under one warp.

Reed — Like a comb, set into the beater frame. Originally made of reeds, now of metal.

Row, pick, throw, shot — A line of weft woven in.

Selvedge (selvage) — The edge at each side of the weaving, where the weft returns around the outside warp.

Sett — Number of warp ends per inch, on the loom.

Shed — The wedge-shaped opening created when alternate warps are raised and lowered. The space where weft yarn travels across the warp.

Shuttle — Holder for a quantity of weft yarn. Slides across the warp, in the shed, carrying the yarn. Many sizes and types for different yarns and uses available, from large wooden rug shuttles to blunt tapestry needles to weave tiny spaces.

Tapestry — Patterned textile. Weft is not thrown the full width of the warp but is manipulated by hand into patterns with many color changes in any row.

Tension — Condition of the warp, which is tied down at each end so threads are taut, allowing the weft to be inserted and beaten down.

Treadles — Pedals that are tied to the harnesses for foot control in raising and lowering of heddles.

Warp — The lengthwise threads fastened to the loom. The foundation of weaving.

Weft — The yarn woven through the warp.

THE ART OF WEAVING, Else Regensteiner. Van Nostrand Reinhold, New York, 1970. A handsome comprehensive handbook for exploring the discipline of fine craftsmanship. Covers looms, weaving, designing, drafting. Extensive glossary and bibliography.

CARD WEAVING OR TABLET WEAVING, Russell E. Groff. Robin and Russ Handweavers, 533 North Adams St., McMinnville, Oregon 97128.

CRAFT YARNS OF RHODE ISLAND, INC. Yarns for Weaving, Knitting and Rug Making, P.O. Box 385, Pawtucket, Rhode Island 02862. Catalog.

FABRICS, Grace G. Denny, Professor Emeritus, University of Washington, Seattle. J. B. Lippincott Co., Philadelphia and New York. Technical and non-technical terms and fabrics are listed alphabetically. This has been an authoritative reference on fabrics since it was first published in 1923. It is now in its eighth edition.

HANDWEAVER AND CRAFTSMAN MAGAZINE, 220 Fifth Ave., New York 10001. A must for weavers. Each issue is full of information on techniques, new books, exhibits, yarns, tools, sources of material, and what weavers all over are up to. Back issues are well worth ordering or looking for in your library. The "Weaver's Bookshelf" section reviews books on all crafts, the arts, design, and any new book that is of interest to craftsmen-designers. We can't say enough in praise of this remarkable magazine, and in praise of the publishers and, the editor, Mary Alice Smith, for providing this publication on textiles.

THE NEW AMERICAN TAPESTRY, Ruth Kaufman. Van Nostrand Reinhold, 1968. A fascinating discussion of contemporary tapestries and woven structures, rich in photographs of work by outstanding American weavers.

SIMPLE WEAVING, Hilary Chetwynd. Watson-Guptil, New York. A small but very informative book.

STEP-BY-STEP WEAVING, Nell Znamierowski Golden Press, New York. Limited, but with brief good information on looms and weaving. Inexpensive.

THE TECHNIQUES OF RUG WEAVING, Peter Collingwood. Watson-Guptil, New York. A very complete book on rug weaving and finishing.

THE TECHNIQUE OF WEAVING, John Tovey. Van Nostrand Reinhold, 1965. A most thorough book for the handweaver wishing to go more thoroughly into the craft. Covers looms, loom preparation, weaving, and specialized techniques.

WEAVING IS FOR ANYONE, Jean Wilson. Van Nostrand Reinhold, 1967. Emphasis is on tapestry weaving techniques and weaving on small devices, with directions for making and weaving on cardboard, frame, circle, backstrap looms. Projects and working drawings for techniques of weaving on looms of all kinds. Contains a good bibliography.

WEAVING WITH CANE AND REED, Grete Kroncke. Van Nostrand Reinhold, 1969. Materials and procedures for making attractive useful baskets. Well illustrated.

West Coast sources

In addition to the bibliographies and supplier lists in the above publications, here are some sources for books, equipment, and yarns on the West Coast. They all publish catalogs.

MAGNOLIA WEAVING (Lillian Hjert), 2635 29th Ave., W., Seattle, Washington 98199.

CRAFT AND HOBBY BOOK SERVICE, Big Sur, California 93920. Their catalogs include just about every book of interest to craftsmen and artists.

ROBIN AND RUSS HANDWEAVERS, 533 North Adams Street, McMinnville, Oregon 97128. Ten times a year they publish WARP AND WEFT, which includes directions for a project, with a woven sample.

THREADS IN ACTION, Box 468, Freeland, Washington 98249. A quarterly featuring directions for macramé and non-loom techniques, and special yarns, beads, tools, new in 1969. Edited and published by Virginia I. Harvey (author of Macramé, Van Nostrand Reinhold, 1967.)

We also suggest U. S. Government pamphlets on specific subjects. You can write to the Library of Congress, Washington, D.C. for lists.

INDEX

Page numbers in italics indicate illustrations.